First World War
and Army of Occupation
War Diary
France, Belgium and Germany

40 DIVISION
Divisional Troops
229 Field Company Royal Engineers
2 June 1916 - 11 June 1919

WO95/2600/2

The Naval & Military Press Ltd
www.nmarchive.com
Published in association with The National Archives

Published by

The Naval & Military Press Ltd

Unit 10 Ridgewood Industrial Park,

Uckfield, East Sussex,

TN22 5QE England

Tel: +44 (0) 1825 749494

www.naval-military-press.com

www.nmarchive.com

This diary has been reprinted in facsimile from the original. Any imperfections are inevitably reproduced and the quality may fall short of modern type and cartographic standards.

© **Crown Copyright**
Images reproduced by permission of The National Archives, London, England, 2015.

Contents

Document type	Place/Title	Date From	Date To
Heading	WO95/2600/2		
Heading	40th Division 229th Field Coy R.E. Jun 1916-Jun 1919		
War Diary	Blackdown	02/06/1916	02/06/1916
War Diary	Havre	03/06/1916	05/06/1916
War Diary	Ligny-Lez-Aires	06/07/1916	06/07/1916
War Diary	Ligny-Lez-Aires	07/06/1916	09/06/1916
War Diary	Mazingarbe	10/06/1916	30/06/1916
Heading	War Diary of 229th Field Company R.E. from 1st July 1916 to 31st July 1916 Vol 2		
War Diary	Bruay	01/07/1916	04/07/1916
War Diary	Les Brebis.	05/07/1916	31/07/1916
Heading	War Diary of 229th Field Coy R.E. from Aug 1st 1916 to Aug 31st 1916 Volume 3		
War Diary	Les Brebis.	01/08/1916	31/08/1916
Heading	War Diary. 229 Field Coy. R.E. From Sept 1st 1916 To Sept 30th 1916 Volume 4 September. 1916		
War Diary	Les Brebis	01/09/1916	30/09/1916
Heading	War Diaries. 229th Field Company. R.E. October 1916. Volume V		
War Diary	Les Brebis	01/10/1916	31/10/1916
Heading	War Diary. 229th Field Company R.E. November 1916. Volume VI		
War Diary	Averdoingt nr. St. Pol.	01/11/1916	02/11/1916
War Diary	Grand Bouret.	03/11/1916	03/11/1916
War Diary	Beauval	04/11/1916	04/11/1916
War Diary	Toutencourt	05/11/1916	19/11/1916
War Diary	Bayencourt	20/11/1916	20/11/1916
War Diary	Halloy	21/11/1916	22/11/1916
War Diary	Orville	23/11/1916	23/11/1916
War Diary	Montrelet	24/11/1916	24/11/1916
War Diary	Yaucourt	25/11/1916	30/11/1916
Heading	War Diary of 229th Field Coy R.E. December, 1916. Volume VII		
War Diary	Yaucourt	01/12/1916	10/12/1916
War Diary	MaurePas Ravine.	11/12/1916	31/12/1916
Heading	War Diary of 229th Field Company R.E. Month of January 1917 Volume VIII		
War Diary	Graniere B. 16.d.8.7	01/01/1917	13/01/1917
War Diary	Cramiere	14/01/1917	25/01/1917
War Diary	Camp 12	26/01/1917	31/01/1917
Heading	A.F.C. 2118 War Diary 229 Field Coy R.E. February 1917 Vol 9		
War Diary	Camp 12 K. 34.a.2.1. (near Bray)	01/02/1917	01/02/1917
War Diary	Sailly-Le-Sec. (Corbie)	02/02/1917	10/02/1917
War Diary	Le Forest B. 16.b.0.3	11/02/1917	14/02/1917
War Diary	Le Forest	14/02/1917	28/02/1917
Heading	229th Field Company R.E. War Diary-Vol 10 March-1917. Vol 10		
War Diary	Le Forest B. 16.B.0.3	01/03/1917	06/03/1917
War Diary	Frise H.13.a.8.6	07/03/1917	18/03/1917

War Diary	Frize.	18/03/1917	31/03/1917
Heading	229th Field Company R.E. War Diary (Vol I). April 1917 Vol XI		
War Diary	Curlu G. 6.b.9.4. Map 62c	01/04/1917	15/04/1917
War Diary	Equancourt V.10.b.3.9. 57c	16/04/1917	18/04/1917
War Diary	Equancourt V.10.b.3.9	19/04/1917	24/04/1917
War Diary	Equancourt	24/04/1917	30/04/1917
Heading	229th Field Co. R.E. War Diary From 1st May 1917. To 31st May 1917. Volume 12		
War Diary	Equancourt	01/05/1917	01/05/1917
War Diary	Dessart Wood W.1.a.9.5	02/05/1917	11/05/1917
War Diary	Heudicourt W. 21.a.2.1	12/05/1917	18/05/1917
War Diary	Heudicourt	19/05/1917	26/05/1917
War Diary	Dessart Wood W. 1.a.9.5	27/05/1917	31/05/1917
Heading	War Diary. 229 Field Coy. R.E. Volume 1 June 1917. Vol 13		
War Diary	Dessart Wood W. 1.a.9.5	01/06/1917	30/06/1917
Heading	War Diary Of 229th Field Company. R.E. Volume 14 July 1917		
War Diary	Dessart Wood. W. 1.a.9.5	01/07/1917	08/07/1917
War Diary	Sunken Road W. 9.d.8.7	09/07/1917	31/07/1917
Heading	War Diary. of 229th Field Company R.E. from 1st August 1917 to 31st August 1917		
War Diary	Sunken Road W. 9.d.8.7	01/08/1917	31/08/1917
Heading	War Diary 229th Field Company Royal Engineers September 17 Vol I		
War Diary	Sunken Road W. 9.d.8.7	01/09/1917	30/09/1917
Heading	War Diary 229th Field Coy. R.E. October 1917 Vol. 17		
War Diary	Sunken Road W. 9.d.8.7	01/10/1917	06/10/1917
War Diary	Sorrel-Le Grand	07/10/1917	07/10/1917
War Diary	Doingt	08/10/1917	11/10/1917
War Diary	Gooy-En. Artois.	12/10/1917	29/10/1917
War Diary	Warden Camp Haut-Allaines C. 29.b.7.7	30/10/1917	31/10/1917
War Diary	Haut Allains	01/11/1917	18/11/1917
War Diary	Barastre	19/11/1917	20/11/1917
War Diary	Beaumetz Lez-Cambrai J.20.a.2.7	21/11/1917	22/11/1917
War Diary	Havrincourt K. 27.b.6.3	23/11/1917	30/11/1917
Heading	War Diary 229th Field Company, Royal Engineers December 1917 Vol 19		
War Diary	Havrincourt. K. 27.b.5.0	01/12/1917	03/12/1917
War Diary	St. Leger	04/12/1917	08/12/1917
War Diary	St. Leger B.4.a.6.8	09/12/1917	28/12/1917
War Diary	St. Leger	29/12/1917	31/12/1917
Heading	229th Field Coy R.E. War Diary-January 1918 Vol. 20		
War Diary	St. Leger.	01/01/1918	13/01/1918
War Diary	St. Leger. T.28.c.7.1	13/01/1918	16/01/1918
War Diary	St. Leger	16/01/1918	31/01/1918
Heading	War Diary. 229th Field Company R.E. February 1918. Vol 21		
War Diary	St. Leger B. 4.a.9.7	01/02/1918	11/02/1918
War Diary	Henin N 32.a.3.4	12/02/1918	28/02/1918
Heading	40th Divisional Engineers 229th Field Company R.E. March 1918		
War Diary	Barley	01/03/1918	02/03/1918
War Diary	Hendicourt	03/03/1918	11/03/1918
War Diary	Boisleux-St. Marc	12/03/1918	21/03/1918

Type	Description	Start	End
War Diary	For A 1a eridently is Meant B 1a	22/03/1918	22/03/1918
War Diary	In Line Sea Behagnies	23/03/1918	24/03/1918
War Diary	Courcelles	25/03/1918	25/03/1918
War Diary	Monchy-Au. Bois.	26/03/1918	26/03/1918
War Diary	Bienvillers.	26/03/1918	26/03/1918
War Diary	Gouy En Artos.	27/03/1918	27/03/1918
War Diary	Sombrin	28/03/1918	31/03/1918
Heading	40th Divisional Engineers. 229th Field Company R.E. April 1918		
Heading	War Diary. 229th Field Company R.E. April 1918. Vol. 22		
Heading	Weekly State of Strength to be Started again 3.5.18		
War Diary	Rue Pruvost.	01/04/1918	01/04/1918
War Diary	Bac St. Maur G. 18.b.8.6	02/04/1918	09/04/1918
War Diary	Bac St. Maur	09/04/1918	10/04/1918
War Diary	Neuf Berquin	10/04/1918	10/04/1918
War Diary	Le. Verrier A. 15.a.5.4	11/04/1918	11/04/1918
War Diary	La Becque Farm A 1.4.b.0.6	11/04/1918	11/04/1918
War Diary	Strazeele.	11/04/1918	13/04/1918
War Diary	Nieppe	14/04/1918	14/04/1918
War Diary	Cormette	15/04/1918	20/04/1918
War Diary	Petit Difques	21/04/1918	24/04/1918
War Diary	St. Sylvestre	24/04/1918	27/04/1918
War Diary	Herzeele D. 20. b. 4.6	28/04/1918	30/04/1918
Heading	229th Field Coy. R.E. War Diary. May 1918 Vol 23		
War Diary	Herzeele D. 14. a. 3.4	01/05/1918	31/05/1918
Miscellaneous	229th Field Coy. R.E. 40th Div. Appendix. A.		
Miscellaneous	Appendix A		
Heading	Appendix A (3)		
Miscellaneous	Appendix A. (4)		
War Diary	Appendix A. (5)		
Heading	229th Field Company R.E. War Diary June 1918 Vol 25		
War Diary	Herzeele. D 14 a. 3.4	01/06/1918	02/06/1918
War Diary	Erskelbrugge B. 25.b.5.4	03/06/1918	23/06/1918
War Diary	Sercus E C 3.d.8.1	23/06/1918	30/06/1918
Miscellaneous	War Diary June 1918. 229th Field Coy. R.E. Appendix. A.	30/06/1918	30/06/1918
Miscellaneous	War Diary. June 1918 229th Field Coy. R.E. Appendix B	30/06/1918	30/06/1918
Miscellaneous	War Diary. June 1918. 229th Field. Coy. R.E. Appendix C	30/06/1918	30/06/1918
Heading	War Diary 229th Field Coy. R.E. July 1918 Vol 26		
War Diary	Sercus C. 3.d.8.1	01/07/1918	31/07/1918
Miscellaneous	Appendix "A"		
Miscellaneous	Appendix "B"	31/07/1918	31/07/1918
Heading	War Diary. 229th Field Company R.E. August 1918 Vol 27		
War Diary	Sercus C.3.d.1.8	01/08/1918	22/08/1918
War Diary	Hazebrouck D.9.b.5.4	23/08/1918	31/08/1918
Miscellaneous	229 Field Coy. R.E. Appendix A.		
Heading	War Diary 229th Field Company R.E. September 1918 Vol-28		
War Diary	La Motte D 30.d.1.4	01/09/1918	01/09/1918
War Diary	Vieux Berquin 36A/E24 b 28	02/09/1918	02/09/1918
War Diary	Le Verrier 36A/F24 c 80	03/09/1918	06/09/1918

War Diary	Le Petit Mortier 36/A 28.b.28	07/09/1918	30/09/1918
Heading	War Diary of 229th Field Co R.E. October 1918 Vol-29		
War Diary	Le Petit Mortier A.28.b.2.8	01/10/1918	05/10/1918
War Diary	Erquinghem H.4.c.6.3	06/10/1918	17/10/1918
War Diary	Perenchies. J. 8.d.7.2	17/10/1918	18/10/1918
War Diary	Wambrechies K.2.b.8.8	18/10/1918	19/10/1918
War Diary	Wambrechies 36/K.2.b.8.8	20/10/1918	23/10/1918
War Diary	Le Molinel	23/10/1918	25/10/1918
War Diary	Nechin 37/H.I.c.7.8	26/10/1918	31/10/1918
Heading	229th Field Coy. R.E. War Diary. Nov. 1918. Vol.		
War Diary	Nechin H. 15.a.0.0	01/11/1918	09/11/1918
War Diary	Pecq 37/1.1.b.49	10/11/1918	14/11/1918
War Diary	Pecq	15/11/1918	15/11/1918
War Diary	Le Molinel 36/F.25.c.8.3	16/11/1918	24/11/1918
War Diary	Le Molinel	26/11/1918	30/11/1918
Diagram etc	Semi-Permanent Bridge. Lille-Tourcoing Road. 37/L.I.d.0.5		
Heading	War Diary 229th Field Company R.E. December 1918 Vol 31		
War Diary	Le Molinel F. 25.c.5.4	01/12/1918	31/12/1918
Heading	War Diary of 229 field Co R.E. January 1919 Vol 32		
War Diary	Le Molinel F. 25.c.5.4	01/01/1919	31/01/1919
Heading	War Diary. 229th Field Co. R.E. February 1919 Vol 29		
War Diary	Le Molinel T.25.c.5.4	01/02/1919	06/02/1919
War Diary	Croix L.q.b.0.3	07/02/1919	28/02/1919
Heading	War Diary. 229th Field Coy. R.E. March 1919. 40 Div Vol 34		
War Diary	Croix L.9.b.0.3	01/03/1919	31/03/1919
Heading	229th Field Co R.E. War Diary April. 1919 Vol 35 40 Div		
War Diary	Croix. L.9.b.0.3	01/04/1919	30/04/1919
Heading	War Diary 229th Field Coy. R.E. May 1919 40 Div Vol 36		
War Diary	Croix 36/L9.b.0.3	01/05/1919	31/05/1919
War Diary	Croix. L9.b.0.3	01/06/1919	11/06/1919

woa5/260/2

40TH DIVISION

229TH FIELD COY R.E.

JUN 1916 - JUN 1919.

Army Form C. 2118

WAR DIARY or INTELLIGENCE SUMMARY
(Erase heading not required.)

229th FIELD Coy. R.E.   Vol 1

Place	Date	Hour	Summary of Events and Information	Remarks and references to Appendices
BLACKDOWN	2.6.16		Company left Camp & Entrain at 7.45 A.m. for SOUTHAMPTON. Arrived at SOUTHAMPTON 9.30 A.M. Embarked for HAVRE and left SOUTHAMPTON DOCKS at 6.30 p.m. by S.S. ARCHIMEDES & S.S. ST TUDNO.	a.S.R. a.S.R.
HAVRE	3.6.16		Disembarked at HAVRE 7.30 A.M. Proceeded to Rest Camp No 5.	a.S.R.
"	4.6.16		Entrained at 7.0 p.m. Left GARE MARITIME. Point 6 9.24 p.m.	a.S.R.
"	5.6.16		Detrained at BERGUETTE at 4.0 p.m. Proceeded to LIGNY-LEZ-AIRES by route march, arriving 7.0 p.m.	a.S.R.
LIGNY-LEZ-AIRES	6.7.16		Billeted in Farms file q.6.16.	a.S.R.
"	7.6.16		Company resting at LIGNY-LEZ-AIRES.	a.S.R.
"	8.6.16		do	a.S.R.
"	9.6.16		do	a.S.R.
			Lieut. J.G. VOCE, R.E. proceeded to MAZINGARBE.	
			At 8.0 A.M. Dismounted men proceeded by Motor-Busses (7) to MAZINGARBE arriving 12.30 p.m. Mounted men and Transport proceed by road to NOEUX-LES-MINES. Billeted in Barns. 2d Lieut R.L. ROLFE & 10 B.R. left at LIGNY-LEZ-AIRES. Proceed on 10th later.	a.S.R.
			Company attached to 16th Division until 26-6-16.	
			2d Lieut R. ROLFE & 10 O.R. proceeded to DRUME2 vs. ESTAIRES for instruction in Hydraulic Rifle work.	
MAZINGARBE	10.6.16		Coy employed on Wiring Revetting of Fire Trenches and Deep Dug-outs at NORTHERN SAP REDOUBT. 36 N.W. 3 G. 23c.	a.S.R.
	11.6.16		do	a.S.R.
	12.6.16		do	a.S.R.
	13.6.16		do	a.S.R.
	14.6.16		do	a.S.R.
	15.6.16		do	a.S.R.
	16.6.16		Work on NORTHERN SAP REDOUBT ceased. Company working in Front line trenches 36 N.W. 3; H 31 a +3 - H 31. c. 6.7.	a.S.R.
	17.6.16		Fixing Equipment Boxes in LOOS WALLERS.	a.S.R.
	18.6.16		As 17.6.16 Fixing Equipment Boxes & LOOS WALLERS. 2d Lieut. J.C. McSHANE wounded at duty (A)	a.S.R.
	19.6.16		No work done. Officers hache over work in MEATH & BRAY TRENCHES from 156 Fd COY R.E.	a.S.R.
	20.6.16		1/1/9 P.C. 1/06. Company working on deep dug outs & Fire Bays in MEATH & BRAY TRENCHES. 36 N.W.3 H.25 a 94.	a.S.R.
	21.6.16		do	a.S.R.
	22.6.16		do	a.S.R.
	23.6.16		do	a.S.R.
	24.6.16		do	a.S.R.
	25.6.16		MEATH & BRAY TRENCHES heavily bombarded by Rifle Grenades & Sulphur shells. Work ceased. 1 N.C.O & 2 men wounded. Order to rejoin 40 Div on 26-6-16 cancelled.	a.S.R.
	26.6.16		Company Employed on Deep Dug Outs in NORTHERN SAP REDOUBT. Continuous work & ships/6.	a.S.R.

Army Form C. 2118

WAR DIARY
or
INTELLIGENCE SUMMARY

(Erase heading not required.) 229th FIELD Co. R.E.

Place	Date	Hour	Summary of Events and Information	Remarks and references to Appendices
MAZINGARBE	27.6.16		Company employed in Deep Dug outs in NORTHERN SAP REDOUBT. Continuous work, 4 reliefs.	aqR
"	28.6.16		do	aqR
"	29.6.16		No work done. Company prepare to rejoin 40' Division on 30.6.16.	aqR
"	30.6.16		Company marched out of MAZINGARBE at 9.30 A.M. and proceeded by Road to BRUAY rejoining 40' Division. Co billeted in Cité 7 of Rue Nationale, BRUAY.	aqR

EWOmulus
Capt. R.E.
O.C. 229th Field Co R.E.
30.6.16

40/ July
229 iFRE
Vol 2

War Diary
229th Field Company R.E.

from 1st July 1916 to 31st July 1916.

WAR DIARY or INTELLIGENCE SUMMARY

Army Form C. 2118

229th FIELD COY. R.E. 40TH DIVISION

JULY 1916

[Stamp: 229th FIELD COMPANY ROYAL ENGINEERS 31 JUL 1916]

Place	Date	Hour	Summary of Events and Information	Remarks and references to Appendices
BRUAY	July 1st	—	Company in Rest Billets (Houses Cité 7). No work done. Physical Exercise and Drill. Gas Helmet Drill.	ASR
"	2nd	—	" " " Orders received to proceed to Les Brebis on 4th inst. to relieve 26th Field Coy R.E. 1st Division	ASR
"	3rd	—	" " " Lieut. J.G. Voce, R.E. proceeds to Les Brebis to take over work from 26th Field Coy. R.E.	ASR
"	4th	—	" " " F.P. Mortimer R.E. Billets	ASR
		2.0 pm	Work on VILLAGE LINE between RAILROAD ALLEY and BOYAU ALLEY, RIGHT SECTOR, 1st ARMY CORPS AREA taken over.	
			Company marched out of BRUAY and proceeded by road to LES BREBIS arriving 7.0 pm. Nos 2 & 4 Sections	ASR
LES BREBIS	5th	—	proceeded to forward Billets. Officers messed with an Village line. No. 1 & No. 3 section billeted in Rue de MAZINGARBE	
"	6th	—	Company dumped work in NORTH MAROC. H.Q.M. 2 N 21.3 section billeted in School in Rue de MAZINGARBE. R.E. Stores collected and Dumps arranged on VILLAGE LINE. One party	ASR
"	7th	—	Company arranged in LES BREBIS. Stores collected and Machine Gun Emplacements repaired on VILLAGE LINE.	ASR
"	8th	—	shelled on way up to trenches. Lieut R.L Rolfe slightly wounded. 1 O.R. badly wounded	ASR
"	9th	—	Company employed on VILLAGE LINE. Drainage of Trenches Repair of Trench boards Rivetting of Traverses Parapets - Firesteps	ASR
"	10th	"	" " "	ASR
"	11th	"	" " " Destruction of Old Boesian stables	ASR
"	12th	"	" " "	ASR
"	13th	"	" " "	ASR
"	14th	"	" " " " Repair CALONNE NORTH Road	ASR
			" employed as above, also Excavating and repairing Deep Dugouts	
"	15th	"	Portion of RESERVE LINE from M.13 to 37 — M 8 d 38 Sheet 36 c SW Fallen over Repair work Stopped	ASR
"	16th	"	Coy Employed on RESERVE & VILLAGE LINES Drainage, repair to French boards, rivetting of Parapets Traverses - Fire Steps. Repair of CALONNE N. Rd	ASR
"	17th	"	Lieut Mortimer proceeds to HOUCHIN for 3 days course of instruction in GAS. Repair of Deep Dug Outs VILLAGE LINE	ASR
"	18th	"	Coy employed on RESERVE & VILLAGE LINES Drainage, Repair to flooring, revetting of Parapets Traverses - FireSteps. Deep dug out - VILLAGE LINE	ASR
"	19th	"	" " " Repair CALONNE NORTH Rd	ASR
"	20th	"	" " " Destruction of old Bombs - Shells	ASR
"	21st	"	" " "	ASR
"	22nd	"	" " " Deep dug out - VILLAGE LINE	ASR
"	23rd	"	" " "	ASR
"	24th	"	" " "	ASR
"	25th	"	" " "	ASR
"	26th	"	" " "	ASR
"	27th	"	" " "	ASR

WAR DIARY or **INTELLIGENCE SUMMARY**
(Erase heading not required.)

Army Form C. 2118

229 Field Co. RE. 40th Division

Place	Date	Hour	Summary of Events and Information	Remarks and references to Appendices
LES BREBIS	July 28	3.30 p.m.	No. 1 & 4 Sections attached to 231st Field Co. RE. to work in Front Line System. Lieut J.C. McSHANE R.E. seriously wounded; one Lance Cpl killed and one Sergeant and few men wounded by accidental explosion in billets. Lieut J.C. McSHANE R.E. died of wounds. Transferred to 33rd Casualty Clearing Station. Evidence of witnesses taken by Lieut A.B. RAYNER R.E. Orders received from C.R.E. to attach No. 2 and 3 Sections to 229th Field Co. RE. to work in LOOS Section.	a.B.R
LES BREBIS	" 29	—	No. 1 Section proceeded to billets in CALONNE. One Section employed on Repair work on RESERVE LINE. Two Sections of 206th Field Co. RE. No. 2 & 3 Sections proceeded to billets in LOOS. 32nd Division attached to 229th Field Co. RE. for work in Reserve.	a.B.R
"	" 30	—	Two attached Sections resting. Clined Parade 3.0 p.m. No work doing in Trenches.	a.B.R
"	" 31	—	Two attached Sections start work on RESERVE LINE from M.13.b.3.7. – M.8.d.3.8. Repair trenches.	a.B.R

E.W. Oundle Capt. R.E.
O.C. 229th Field Co. R.E.

31-7-16.

No. 3

CONFIDENTIAL

WAR DIARY

of 5 Field Coy RE

229th Field Coy RE to Aug 31st 1916

from Aug 1st 1916   VOLUME 3

Army Form C. 2118

WAR DIARY or INTELLIGENCE SUMMARY

(Erase heading not required.)

229TH FIELD COY. R.E. 40TH DIVISION

AUGUST 1916.

Place	Date	Hour	Summary of Events and Information	Remarks and references to Appendices
LES BREBIS	Aug. 1st		Two attached Sections of 206th Field Coy. RE employed on revetting & repairing in RESERVE LINE between M.13.b.3.7. & M.8.d.3.8. Casualties Wounded O.R. 1 in No. 2 Sect. – attached to 2nd 1st Field Coy. R.E.	a3R
"	" 2nd		Two attached Sections Employed repairing in RESERVE LINE as above. Casualties Wounded O.R. 1 in W83	a3R
"	" 3rd		Section attached to 2nd Field Coy. R.E. Instructions received from C.R.E. 32nd Div. that the CRE. 40th Div. & the two Sections of 206 FD.CoRE. & proceed to BEUVRY EAST on afternoon of 3rd Aug. No trench work done. Casualties Wounded O.R. 1 in No. 3 Sect. attached 206 FD.C.RE.	a3R
"	" 4th		Wound believed to be self-inflicted. Enquiry instituted. 2.0 P.M. Two section 206 FD Coy march out to BEUVRY. 2nd Lieut. E.F. BORRIE R.E. joined company from BASE.	a3R
"	" 5th		2nd Lieut. E.F. BORRIE R.E. proceed to LOOS to take over command of No. 3 Section. Detail 1 Company employed in Company work shop – Together with 12 attached men from 120" Inf Bgde – and 2 improvement of billets. New Lines in LES BREBIS.	a3R
"	" 6th		Details employed in Coy. Workshop	a3R
"	" 7th		" "	a3R
"	" 8th		" " . Inspection of M.G. Emplacements in VILLAGE LINE	a4R
"	" 9th		Church Parade 3.0 P.M.	a4R
"	" 10th		No. 3 – 24 Sections return to Coy. from LOOS at 11.30 P.M.	a4R
"	" 11th		No. 3 – 24 Sections resting.	a4R
"	" 12th		No. 2 – 3 Sections revetting & drainage in VILLAGE and RESERVE LINES	a4R
"	" 13th		No. 2 . 3 & 4 Sections working in VILLAGE & RESERVE LINES	a4R
"	" 14th		" "	a4R
"	" 15th		No. 1 Section returned from CALONNE to LES BREBIS rejoins company. No. 4 also rejoins company. No. 3 " proceeded to forward billets in MARO C.	N4R
"	" 16th		No. 2 – 3 Sections working in VILLAGE & RESERVE LINES. No. 1 & 4 Sections resting.	a3R
"	" 17th		No. 1 . 2 . 3 & 4 Sections working in VILLAGE . RESERVE LINES. Cabourne Sector. Revetting, draining & dugouts	a3R
"	" 18th		" "	a3R
"	" 19th		Work on deep dugouts in ALGIERS TRENCH M20 & A1 commenced. Billets in LES BREBIS shelled during afternoon. No damage done to Coy. Billets.	a3R
"	" 20th		Company work in VILLAGE . RESERVE LINES and ALGIERS TRENCH. Dugouts, revetting & draining	a3R

Army Form C. 2118

WAR DIARY or INTELLIGENCE SUMMARY
(Erase heading not required.)

229th FIELD Cy R.E. 40th DIVISION

Title Pages. AUGUST 1916.

Place	Date	Hour	Summary of Events and Information	Remarks and references to Appendices
LES BREBIS	Aug 21		Coy employed on repair work & deep dug outs on VILLAGE & RESERVE LINES, Deep dug outs in ALGIERS TRENCH and deep dug outs in HORSE GUARDS AVENUE, M.15.a.5.4. 4 Reinforcements from Base.	asR
"	22		"	asR
			11 Lieut R.L ROLFE, R.E. and party of Sappers took part in the Bombing Raid on Enemy trenches at M. 20 b 2.0. Superintended the carry of the Bangalore Torpedoes under enemy wire and exploding it – at 10.50 P.M.	
"	23		Coy employed on repair work & deep dug outs on VILLAGE & RESERVE LINES, Deep dug outs in ALGIERS TRENCH & HORSE GUARDS AVENUE. Orders received to take over the LOOS Sector. All work stopped at 8.0 P.M. on MAROC & CALONNE Sectors.	asR
"	24		Officers took over LOOS Section. No. 2 Section moved to billets in LOOS.	asR
"	25		No. 4 Section proceed to Billets in LOOS. 2 officers and 106 other ranks of 119th Inf Bgde attached to Company as permanent working party, as from I.N.C.O. 2. 25 men of each of 19" R.W.F., 12" S.W.B. "17" Welch, 18" Welch.	asR
"	26		Work commenced on LOOS SECTOR. 2 section on consolidation of Craters, and construction of dug outs. 2 section on Tunnel maintenance.	asR
"	27		do	asR
"	28		do	asR
"	29		do	asR
"	30		do	asR
"	31		do	asR

EWThurston
Capt. R.E.
OC 229th Field Co R.E.

Vol 4

CONFIDENTIAL.

WAR DIARY.

229 FIELD COY. R.E.

From Sept 1st 1916.   To Sept 30th 1916

VOLUME 4

SEPTEMBER. 1916.

WAR DIARY or INTELLIGENCE SUMMARY

Army Form C. 2118

229th FIELD Coy R.E. 40th DIVISION

Title Pages SEPTEMBER. 1916.

Place	Date	Hour	Summary of Events and Information	Remarks and references to Appendices
LES BREBIS	Sept 1st		Coy Hd. Qrs. billeted in LES BREBIS. 4 Sections in LOOS. 2 Sections employed on consolidation of craters and construction of dug outs, 2 Section on Trench maintenance, dug outs, Trench Mortar & Lewis Gun Emplcmts.	AGR
"	2nd		do	AGR
"	3rd		do	
"	4th		Enemy blew small camouflet near SEAFORTH CRATER M.6.b.9.6. at 8.0 p.m. Parties of Sappers opening & new sap dug from Front Line to near lip of Crater & filling in Gaps & part of Front Line trench. 2 Section on Crater consolidation & deep dug outs; 2 Section on Trench maintenance dug outs, T.M. & L.G. Emplcmts. New saps constructed from Front Line to SEAFORTH CRATER	AGR
"	5th		do	AGR
"	6th		do	AGR
"	7th		do	
"	8th		3 NCO's & 36 men of 13th Welsh Regt. attached for work on Stokes & T.M. Emplacements until 11th inst. 1 Section Employed on dug outs and general Trench work. 1 Section on Craters and deep dug outs. Trench mortar Emplacements, Machine & Stokes Gun Emplacements.	AGR
"	9th		do	AGR
"	10th		do	AGR
"	11th		121st Inf. Bgde relieve 119 Bgde in LOOS Sector. Work on dug outs continued with a few men. Remainder resting. Attached infantry parties changed. Following parties attached for work on Craters: 10 OR. 13th Yorks. 14. 81 OR. 20 Suffolks. 14 OR. 34 OR. 21st Middlesex.	AGR
"	12th		4 Sections & attached Infantry working on Crater consolidation, deep dug outs, Trench mortar & Stokes Gun & Machine Gun Emplacement & general trench maintenance. WREXHAM TUNNEL being repaired.	AGR
"	13th		do	AGR
"	14th		do	AGR
"	15th		do	AGR
"	16th		do	AGR
"	17th		do	AGR
"	18th		do	AGR

WAR DIARY
or
INTELLIGENCE SUMMARY

(Erase heading not required.)

SEPTEMBER, 1916.   **229th FIELD COY. R.E.   40th DIVISION.**

Army Form C. 2118

Place	Date	Hour	Summary of Events and Information	Remarks and references to Appendices
LES BREBIS	Sept.19		4 Sections and attached Infantry working on Consolidation of Craton (SEAFORTH, CAMERON & HARTS) deep dugouts - Heavy Medium & Light Trench Mortar Emplacements - Trench Drainage Scheme, General Trench Maintenance	Q.B.R.
"	" 20		do	Q.B.R.
"	" 21		Lieut. F.P. MORTIMER R.E. wounded at Harrison's Crater. Lieut MORTIMER evacuated. Sections and attached Infantry working on Consolidation of Crater (SEAFORTH CAMERONS HARTS); deep dug outs. Heavy, Medium & Light Trench Mortar Emplacements. Trench Drainage Scheme. General Trench Maintenance	Q.B.R.
"	" 22		do	Q.B.R.
"	" 23		do	Q.B.R.
"	" 24	11-10p	2/Lieut R.L. Rolfe R.E. + party of Sappers & Infantry raid two Bangalore torpedoes under enemy wire, exploded the wire. Raid was not made accessible. Enemy wire exploded the gap was formed as required. at M6 b 42 & M6 b 31. Sections & attached Infantry working as in 23rd Inst.	Q.B.R.
		2.30a	Mine Bomb at 6.½ vee R.E. superintended entry & two Bangalore torpedoes under enemy wire. Torpedoes blown at 10p.m. 2 required gaps made 2/Lieut LESLIE R.E. reported for duty's given command no.2 Section	Q.B.R.
"	" 25		Sections & attached Infantry employed as on 21st Inst. 2 Sappers & 1 mine (Reinforcements) reported	Q.B.R.
		2.3p	Mine blown at M6 b 6.7 2/Lieut F.F.BORRIE R.E. Raid consolidation party on tr near Cpy. Bomber. pits 1 Sapper evacuated under fire in daylight. 1 O.R. Wounded. Further Consolidation of upper.	Q.B.R.
"	" 26		Sections and attached Infantry working on Consolidation of Crater (SEAFORTH CAMERON'S & SHOREDITCH) deep dug outs, Heavy, Medium & Stokes gun Emplacements - Trench Drainage Scheme - General Trench Maintenance	Q.B.R.
"	" 27		do	Q.B.R.
"	" 28		do	Q.B.R. 1 O.R. Wounded Shock Shell
"	" 29		do	Q.B.R.
"	" 30		do	Q.B.R.

E.W. Orwater? Capt. RE
O.C. 229th Field Co.y R.E.
30.9.16.

CONFIDENTIAL

WAR DIARIES

229th Field Company. R.E.

October 1916.

VOLUME V

INTELLIGENCE SUMMARY

229th FIELD COY. R.E. 40th DIVISION

OCTOBER 1916. (Erase heading not required.)

Place	Date	Hour	Summary of Events and Information	Remarks and references to Appendices
LES BREBIS	Oct 1st	—	Company Headquarters billeted in LES BREBIS. Sections in LOS. 4 officers and 273 O.R. attached for work. Sections and attached men working on Crater Consolidation T.M. & M.G. Emplacements Dugouts. 2 Trench Maintenance and Drainage. 3 Bangalore Torpedoes blown under Enemy wire at M.6.d.6.9. Gaps formed.	A&R
"	2	—	Sections and attached men working on Crater consolidation T.M. & M.G. Emplacements Dugouts Drainage Trench Maintenance	A&R
"	3	—	do	A&R
"	4	—	3 Bangalore Torpedoes blown under Enemy wire at H.31.c.4.1. Gaps formed. Sections and attached men working on Crater consolidation T.M. & Stokes Emplacements Dugouts Drainage Trench Maintenance	A&R
"	5	—	do	A&R
"	6	—	Bangalore Torpedoes blown under Enemy wire at M.6.b.2.0. at 12.30am. Gaps formed. 1 O.R. killed by shell. Sections & attached men working on Crater Consolidation T.M. & Stokes Emplacements Dugouts Drainage Trench Maintenance	A&R
"	7	—	do	A&R
"	8	—	4 Bangalore Torpedoes blown under Enemy wire near sap M.5.d.5.5. Gaps formed. Trench work as on 7th. 3 Bangalore Torpedoes blown under Enemy wire at M.6.b.5.3. Party bombed back twice but fired fuze of third attempt.	A&R
"	9	—	Sections & attached men working on Crater consolidation T.M. Stokes Emplacements Dugouts Drainage Trench Maintenance. Trench work as on 9th. No.1 Section returns to Rest Billets in LES BREBIS.	A&R
"	10	—	do No.3 " " "	A&R
"	11	—	Right Sub Sector M.5.d.3.9. to M.6.b.5.6. Sheet 36c SW. Now Runs over to 224th Field Co. RE. 1st Bus Sector from H.31.a.0.5 to H.25.b.23. Taken over from 231st Field Co RE. Company now hold 1st Bis Section.	C&R
"	12	—	Small mine blown near SEAFORTH CRATER at M.6.9.b. No crater formed. Damaged Saps Dugouts part repaired. Sections & attached men working on Crater consolidation T.M. Stokes Emplacements Dugouts Drainage Trench Maintenance	A&R
"	13	—	do	A&R
"	14	—	do	A&R
"	15	—	do	A&R
"	16	—	Enemy blew Small mine at SEAFORTH CRATER M.6.9.6. at 12.30p.m. 70 yds fire fire field. Also Saps bombing posts. New sap dug towards posts constructed. Rear line cleared before engineer. Trench work as on 12th. No.1 Section returns to billets in LES BREBIS. 5 Sections duty in line	A&R

WAR DIARY or INTELLIGENCE SUMMARY

229TH FIELD COY R.E.   40TH DIVISION

OCTOBER 1916.

Place	Date	Hour	Summary of Events and Information	Remarks and references to Appendices
LES BREBIS	Oct 17	—	Sections 2 attached men working on Crater Consolidation, T.M. & Stokes Emplacement, Dug outs, Drainage & Trench maintenance. No. 3 Section return to billets in LES BREBIS & resuming duties – Re Cmdt.	ASR
"	18	—	Sections attached men working on Crater consolidation, T.M. Emplacements, Dug outs, Drainage & Trench Maintenance	ASR
"	19	—	do	ASR
"	20	—	do	ASR
"	21	—	Trench work as on 18" 1 O.R. Employed at No 1 Ord. Mob. Workshops return for duty	ASR
"	22	—	do Corps Workshops	ASR
"	23	—	Sections and attached men on Crater consolidation, T.M. & Stokes Emplace'ts, Dug outs, Drainage, Trench Maintenance	ASR
"	24	—	do	ASR
"	25	—	do	ASR
"	26	—	do	ASR
"	27	—	Advance Party of 104" Field Coy R.E. — 2 Offs. 10 NCOs arrive to take over billets & Stables. Trench work for two sections as on 23" — 2 Offs. 2 Sections return to billets in LES BREBIS. 104" Field Coy R.E. mainO's at 11.0 p.m. Work – 14 O/Ts Section new huts. Handed over to O/C 104 Field Coy R.E.	ASR
"	28	—	Two sections return to billets in LES BREBIS. All attached infantry return to 121" Brigade. Company resting in LES BREBIS.	ASR
"	29	12.30	Company marches to BRUAY arriving 4.20 p.m. Billetty party go to BRUAY	ASR
"	30	9.30 am	" – " – " – AVERDOINGT near St Pol, arriving at 6.0 p.m. Billetted in BRUAY	ASR
"	31	—	" resting in AVERDOINGT	ASR

C.B.Rampton
Lieut. R.E.
for O/C 229" Field Coy R.E.

Confidential.

Vol 6

WAR DIARY.
229th Field Company R.E.

November 1916.

VOLUME VI

WAR DIARY
or
INTELLIGENCE SUMMARY

(Erase heading not required.)

229TH FIELD Cy R.E.

NOVEMBER 1916.

Place	Date	Hour	Summary of Events and Information	Remarks and references to Appendices
AVERDOINGT nr. ST. POL.	Nov. 1st		Map Reference 1/100,000 FRANCE. LENS. Coy in rest billets in 120th Infantry Bgde. billetting area. Billetted in farms.	A.C.R.
do	2nd		Company marches out of AVERDOINGT at 9.30 P.M. through MAGNICOURT & REBREUVIETTE to GRAND BOURET. Billetted in farms.	A.C.R.
GRAND BOURET.	3rd		Company marches out of GRAND BOURET at 11.15 A.M. through FRÉVENT BOUQUEMAISON & DOULLENS to BEAUVAL. Company reverts to 40th DIVISION. Is proceeded to 5th Army Head Quarters.	A.C.R.
BEAUVAL	4th		Company marches out of BEAUVAL & proceeds through BEAUQUESNE & P to TOUTENCOURT. Company to in Camp at TOUTENCOURT and is attached to Head Quarters 5th Army.	A.C.R.
TOUTENCOURT	5th		Company resting.	
"	6th		" Company Employed on erecting huts, repairing & removing huts	A.C.R.
"	7th		do do	A.C.R.
"	8th		do do	A.C.R.
"	9th		do do	A.C.R.
"	10th		do do	A.C.R.
"	11th		do do	A.C.R.
"	12th		do do	A.C.R.
"	13th		do do	A.C.R.
"	14th		1 Warrant officer evacuated	A.C.R.
"	15th		Company in Camp at TOUTENCOURT & employed in erecting huts, garage, repairing & removing huts.	A.C.R.
"	16th		do do	A.C.R.
"	17th		Orders received to proceed to BAYENCOURT on 19th inst. to join the XIII Corps as Corps Troops	A.C.R.

WAR DIARY
or
INTELLIGENCE SUMMARY

Army Form C. 2118

229th FIELD Co RE.

NOVEMBER 1916

Place	Date	Hour	Summary of Events and Information	Remarks and references to Appendices
TOUTENCOURT	Nov. 18		Company employed on erecting huts & repairing & removing huts. Preparation made to move on 19th	APR
"	19		Dismounted men proceed - Motor buses to BAYENCOURT started 1.30p. Mounted men & transport proceed by road leaving at 10.30 a.m. arrived at BAYENCOURT 2.0 p.m.	APR
BAYENCOURT	20		Orders received at 12.30 p.m. to proceed to HALLOY on 20th inst. Company leaves BAYENCOURT at 9.45 p.m. proceeds by march route to HALLOY (van DOUBSM) Company billeted in huts.	APR
HALLOY.	21		Company - HALLOY. Drill and inspection. Orders of reading	APR
"	22		to proceed to ORVILLE on 22nd.	
ORVILLE	23		Company proceeds by march route to ORVILLE. Billetted = farms.	APR
MONTRELET	24		Company proceeds by march route to MONTRELET.	APR
YAUCOURT	25		- YAUCOURT near ABBEVILLE. (MAP ABBEVILLE 1/4 scale 1/100,000) Company on fatigue work cleaning billets making latrines estimating &c.	APR
"	26		- - Drill.	APR
"	27		Coy. Training. (1st & 2nd Weeks). Overhaul of Arms, Harness, Vehicles. Squad Drill, Musketry Exercises + Physical Training. Improvement of billets in Brigade area.	APR
"	28		Do	
"	29		Do	
"	30		Do	

E.W. Orr..... Major R.E.
Commanding 229 F.C. R.E.

Confidential

War Diary
of
229th Field Coy R.E.

December, 1916. Volume VII

WAR DIARY
or
INTELLIGENCE SUMMARY

(Erase heading not required.)

229 FIELD COY R.E. 40 DIV.

Army Form C. 2118

DECEMBER 1916

Reference Map ABBEVILLE 1/100,000

Place	Date	Hour	Summary of Events and Information	Remarks and references to Appendices
YAUCOURT	Dec 1		Company on Physical Training, Drill and Improvement of Billets in 120' by Bgde Area	AGR
	2		do	AGR
	3		do	AGR
	4		do	AGR
	5		do	AGR
	6		do	AGR
	7		Four O.R. join from Base	
	8		2Lieut T. Hudson joins Company. Company on Physical Training, Drill & Billet Improvement. Transport and mounted Personnel Leave YAUCOURT and proceed by march route to ARGOEUVRES	AGR
	9		Dismounted personnel proceed by road route (from REMY near ABBEVILLE) and hence by train to MERICOURT; detraine and proceed by march route to BIELETS & BRAY.	AGR
	10		Transport & mounted personnel proceed by march route from ARGOEUVRES to BRAY. Company proceed by march route from BRAY to MAUREPAS RAVINE. One O.R. died at BRAY.	AGR AGR
BRAY				
MAUREPAS RAVINE	11		Company in Tents in MAUREPAS RAVINE. Coy attached to 4 Div for rations	OUR
	12		Company repairing & improving billets. Work on INTERMEDIATE line later working up work allowed to sections	LGR AGR
	13		do. do. Silos chosen for erection.	AGR
	14		Coys take over Pumping stations.	AGR
	15		Work started on INTERMEDIATE LINE, Machine Gun Dug Outs & Wiring of line	AGR AGR
	16		Work on INTERMEDIATE LINE do do	AGR AGR
	17			
	18		Company move into new billets (dugouts) near MAUREPAS RAVINE. Work on INTERMEDIATE Line. Machine Gun Dug Outs & Wiring of line	AGR AGR

WAR DIARY
or
INTELLIGENCE SUMMARY

(Erase heading not required.)

229ᵈ Field Coy R.E.   40ᵗʰ Divn.

Reference: Sheet 62ᵈ N.W. 1/40,000
FRANCE

Place	Date	Hour	Summary of Events and Information	Remarks and references to Appendices
MAUREPAS RAVINE.	Dec 19 - 20		Work on INTERMEDIATE LINE. Dug outs and Wiring Ihure.	C.R.E.
	21		Wiring of line completed. Dug outs levelled over to Tunnelling Coys R.E. Erection of Nissen huts commenced.	C.R.E.
	22		" " " "	C.R.E.
	23		do	C.R.E.
	24		do	C.R.E.
	25		Company resting.	
	26		" " Officers take over work from 33ʳᵈ Divisional R.E. in Right Sector.	C.R.E.
			Company takes over Right sector, moves into billets near LE FOREST. Two sections proceed to billets at ANDOVER. Cy. Hd. Qrs. at B.17.a.1.3.	C.R.E.
	27		Compys. working on communication trenches, cleaning, draining dug outs, construction of Gun Belt Stove etc. Construction of Machine Gun dug outs. (Repair of)	C.R.E.
	28		do	C.R.E.
	29		do	C.R.E.
	30		do	C.R.E.
	31		do	C.R.E.

A.B. Rampton Lieut. R.E.
[illegible] 229ᵗʰ Field Coy R.E.

Confidential

Vol 8

War Diary
of
229th Field Company R.E.

month of January 1917

VOLUME VIII

Army Form C. 2118

WAR DIARY or INTELLIGENCE SUMMARY

(Erase heading not required.)

229th FIELD Coy R.E.   40TH DIVISION.

Instructions regarding War Diaries and Intelligence Summaries are contained in F.S. Regs., Part II. and the Staff Manual respectively. Title Pages will be prepared in manuscript.

Place	Date	Hour	Summary of Events and Information	Remarks and references to Appendices
GRANIERE. B.1.b.8.7.	JAN.1st		REFERENCE. FRANCE. (ALBERT) 62 C N.W. 1/20,000. ED. 3B.	
			Coy Head Quarters & 2 Sections in town. Billets at ANDOVER C.13.a.3.6. Transport and mounted personnel at "Y" Wood A.23.d.5.7.	aSR
			Coy employed on clearing & draining communication trenches, construction of dug outs. Repair of Baths. 2 BAn. Hd Qrs.	aSR
	2nd		Work as on 1st. Construction of deviation track (Tent'd roots) round bad places in trench.	aSR
	3		do	aSR
	4		Repair of 0.40 m track to ANDOVER. Track used for transport of R.E. Stores.	aSR
	5		do	aSR
	6		as on 1st.	aSR
	7		Work as on 1st. Sinking of well at ANDOVER for water supply.	aSR
	8		Work at ANDOVER. Sinking well, constructing Gumboot shed. Garrison 2 A.P.M & Dugouts. Repairing OP BAO.HdQrs. Draining valley and repairing path by billet.	aSR
			Work at GRANIERE. Demolishing duck board track & roads over. Repair to Rgt. Bgde Hd Qrs. Coy Workshop established. Constructing things for water carrying. Wire bunds etc.	aSR
	8		do	aSR
	9		do	aSR
	10		2 Latrines being constructed at ANDOVER. 40cm railway used for conveying Restos to ANDOVER A.D.S. at ALDERSHOT LINE o at GRANIERE being repaired.	aSR
	11		do	aSR
	12		do	aSR
			as on 7th but duck board track ANDOVER complete. track shifted 8m between	aSR
			CAMP to ALDERSHOT.	aSR
	13		as on 12th. Repair to Pumping Station at GRANIERE.	aSR

WAR DIARY or INTELLIGENCE SUMMARY

Army Form C. 2118

(Erase heading not required.) 22nd Field Coy. R.E. 40th Div. Sigs.

January 1917.

Place	Date	Hour	Summary of Events and Information	Remarks and references to Appendices
CRAMERIE	14		Work as on 12th Inst.	R.W.P.
	15		——do——	R.W.P.
	16		——Do——	R.W.P.
	17		——Do—— Andover Place Gas - Shelled from 9.0 P.M. to 11.0 P.M.	R.W.P.
	18		——Do——	R.W.P.
	19		——Do—— Andover Place Gas - Shelled from 8.0 P.M. to 11.0 P.M.	R.W.P.
	20		——Do—— No. 4 Section relieved No 1 Sect at Andover Place.	R.W.P.
	21		——Do——	R.W.P.
	22		——Do—— Buckboard Track to Agile Trench from Brig. H.Q. completed.	R.W.P.
	23		——Do—— Cramiere Water Station wired.	R.W.P.
	24		——Do—— 1 Dugout completed.	R.W.P.
	25		Coy. Relieved by (8th Div.) 9th Field Coy. R.E. Accommodate 70 men.	R.W.P.
	26		Coy. Rest. Collecting Material. 15th (IWR) Field Coy. R.E. Proceeded to Campie.	R.W.P.
CAMPIE	27		Coy. employed on improvements to billets. Campie.	R.W.P.
	28		——Do——	R.W.P.
	29		——Do——	R.W.P.
	30		——Do——	R.W.P.
	31		——Do——	R.W.P.

Signed
OC. 22nd Field Coy R.E.

Vol 9

CONFIDENTIAL

A.F. C2118. WAR DIARY

229 FIELD COY R.E.

FEBRUARY 1917.

Army Form C. 2118

WAR DIARY
or
INTELLIGENCE SUMMARY

(Erase heading not required.) 229TH FIELD COY R.E. 40TH DIVISION.

FEBRUARY 1917.

REF. ALBERT (Combined Sheet) 57c S.E. / 57c S.W. / 62c N.E. / 62d N.W. & BOUCHAVESNES. 62c N.W.2.

Place	Date	Hour	Summary of Events and Information	Remarks and references to Appendices
CAMP 12 K.34.a.2.1. (near BRAY)	Feb. 1st		Coy Headquarters & 2 Sections proceed to SAILLY-LE-SEC (J 23 & 29.) to undertake Billet improvements in 119 & 121 Inf. Bgde Areas. in billets in SAILLY-LE-SEC.	over
	2nd		No 3 Section proceeds to CHIPILLY (62D S.E. Q.4.) with transport to undertake Billet improvements for 119-121 Inf Bgde units in Camp 12. in billets	over
	3		No 1 Section proceeds to CORBIE (62D N.W. 1.) for Billet improvements - 120 Inf Bgde Area. in Billets	over
SAILLY-LE-SEC (CORBIE)			Billet Improvements - 120, 119-121 Inf Bgde Areas commenced. Transport being overhauled	over
			do	over
	4		Billet improvements in SAILLY-LAVIETTE & Camp 124. Also in A+B lines Camp 12 & CHIPILLY & CORBIE. Overhauling of Transport, harness & equipment. Major E.W. ORMSTON returns from R.E. Arms at LE PARQ.	over
	5		do as on 4th.	over
	6		do	over
	7		do	over
	8		do also Rifle and Squad Drill.	over
	9		do	over
	10th		No 1 Section rejoins Coy at SAILLY-LE-SEC. Coy proceeds by march route to Camp 21. Officers and party take over quarters at LE FOREST RANCOURT SECTOR	over
LE FOREST B.16.b.0.3.	11		Coy proceeds to LE FOREST and takes over the RANCOURT SECTOR. Officers take over work	over
	12		Coy working on Day duty, maintenance of Tramlines, Duckboard Tracks, area entrenchments of Posts in front lines, improvement and opening up of Communication Trenches, supervision of wiring, also Brigade pour improvements of Bgde & Battn. Hd Qrs etc. Construction of Aid Posts.	over
	13		Work as on 12th Inst. Construction & Stokes Bomb Store.	
	14		do	

Army Form C. 2118

WAR DIARY
or
INTELLIGENCE SUMMARY

(Erase heading not required.)

229th FIELD COY RE 40th DIVISION

FEBRUARY 1917

MAP. BOUCHAVESNES 62c N.W.2.

Place	Date	Hour	Summary of Events and Information	Remarks and references to Appendices
L'te FOREST.	14	12 mdt.	Work in line etc. as on 12th. Two reinforcements supplied.	CWSR
	15	12"	Work in line etc. as on 12th. Construction of Dugouts for Infantry Battn. Wiring front line etc.	CWSR
	16	12.5	Work in line etc. as on 12th. Supervising work in Quellen trenches. Engineer's Parkleen O.P.	CWSR
	17	16"	Work in line etc. as on 16th. Seven reinforcements supplied.	CWSR
	18	16"		
	19	16"	Work in line as on 16th.	CWSR
	20	"	Work in line as on " 1 O.R. wounded.	"
	21	"	Work in line as on " 16 mdt. Improvement of Shelters at LE FOREST. Construction of Strong Points.	CWSR
	22	"	Work additional Shelter Kuka on 21st. 8" Div. from C.9, C.10, B.A, to C.9 to A.4.	CWSR
	23	"	Work — line as on 21st. Reinf.	CWSR
	24		Work — line as on 21st	CWSR
	25		Work — line as on 21	CWSR
	26		Work — line as on 21st	CWSR
	27		Work — line as on 21st	CWSR
	28		Work — line as on 21st	CWSR

C.B. Rayner
Capt. R.E.
for MAJOR R.E.
COMMDG. 229th FIELD COMPANY R.E.

Vol 10

CONFIDENTIAL

229th FIELD COMPANY R.E.

WAR DIARY - VOL. 10

MARCH - 1917.

WAR DIARY or INTELLIGENCE SUMMARY

Army Form C. 2118

(1)

229 FIELD Cᵒʸ R.E. 40 DIVISION

MARCH 1917.

Place	Date	Hour	Summary of Events and Information	Remarks and references to Appendices
LE FOREST B.16.b.0.3	MAR 1ˢᵗ		BOUCHAVESNES 62 C. N.W.2. 2. 62 C N.W. LE FOREST. Working in RANCOURT SECTOR work on dug outs maintenance from line - Drill - several trenches in area construction of different posts in Front line. Improvement and opening up of communication superservice trench along Brigade Front. Construction of A.D. posts etc. Work in line as on 1ˢᵗ inst.	CRR
	2		Work in line as on 1ˢᵗ inst.	CRR
	3		Work in line as on 1ˢᵗ inst.	CRR
	4		Work in Cup reserve owing to attack by 8ᵗʰ Div. on Right flank. Work resumed in afternoon.	CRR
	5		Work in line as on 1ˢᵗ inst. Advance fully told our sides ate at FRISE fm 212.4 N.25C.14.	CRR
	6		Company relieved by 2ⁿᵈ Field Cᵒ. Work handed over. Company proceeds by march route to FRISE & becomes R.E. Cᵒ = Divisional Reserve.	CRR
FRISE H.13.a.B.6.	7		Company employed on road repair, camouflage of roads, erection of huts in Camp 19. SUZANNE maintenance of WURZEL AVE to Bgde Headquarters PC WURZEL.	CRR
	8		Work as on 7.	CRR
	9		Work as on 7.	CRR
	10		Work as on 7.	CRR
	11		Work as on 7.	CRR
	12		Work as on 7.	CRR
	13		Work as on 7.	CRR
	14		Work in SUZANNE Camp 19 ceased. Company employed on road repair & drainage & enlargement of Roads & maintenance of WURZEL AVE. W.P.C. WURZEL.	CRR
	15		Work as on 14.	CRR
	16		Work as on 14.	CRR
	17		Work as on 14.	CRR
	18.		Germans evacuated PERONNE at 1.15 P.m. Troops moved forwards. 2ⁿᵈ Lieut. R.L. ROLFE marched FLAMICOURT at 1.50 P.m. DOINGT at 3.0 P.m.	CRR

Army Form C. 2118

WAR DIARY
or
INTELLIGENCE SUMMARY

(Erase heading not required.)

229th FIELD Co R.E. 40th DIVISION.

MARCH 1917.

Place	Date	Hour	Summary of Events and Information	Remarks and references to Appendices
FRIZE.	18		Lieut. R.L. ROLFE R.E. reported on town. Revetted etc. Company employed on bridging, trenches & road repairs on main PERONNE Road.	aBR
	19		Work as on 18. Erection of water points. Reconnaissance of huts & bridges.	aBR
	20		Work as on 19. Water Supply - MONT ST QUENTIN	cBR
	21		Work as on 19. Reconnaissance of road to BRIECOURT.	aBR
	22		Company moved into billets in CLERY. Work as on 19.	aBR
	23		Work as on 19. Repair of CLERY - FEUILLAUCOURT Road.	aBR
	24		Work as on 19. do	aBR
	25		Division withdrawn from line. Company moved back to CURLU.	aBR
	26		Company employed on MARICOURT - PERONNE Railway & road diversion, construction of bridge on CLERY - PERONNE Road.	aBR
	27		Work as on 26.	
	28		Work as on 26.	
	29		Work as on 26. Reconstn. of PERONNE Rd nr VENDELU.	aBR
	30		do	
	31		Work as on 26. Repair of CLERY - FEUILLAUCOURT RD.	aBR aBR

O.B.Rennie Capt R.E f. MAJOR R.E.
COMMDG. 229th FIELD COMPANY R.E.

CONFIDENTIAL

229th FIELD COMPANY R.E. XI

WAR DIARY (VOL I).

APRIL 1917

WAR DIARY
or
INTELLIGENCE SUMMARY

(Erase heading not required.)

229th FIELD CO R.E.   40th DIVISION.

APRIL 1917.

Place	Date	Hour	Summary of Events and Information	Remarks and references to Appendices
CURLU 6.b.b.9.4. Map 62c	APRIL 1st		Company Head Quarters and Transport at CURLU and employed on MARICOURT-PERONNE RAILWAY, clearing culverts, repairing old trench tramway under formation and draining embankments. Work on Railway ceased at 4.0 p.m. Two Sections billeted in dug-outs at CLERY H.5 c.59. Proceed to MARICOURT. Nissen Huts on site chosen for DIVISIONAL H.Q. V13.c 62. Map 57c. 4 O.R. join Co. from Bn. 2. 1 O.R. admitted to hospital accidentally injured.	O.B.R.
"	" 2		Two sections with section transport proceed from CLERY to MARICOURT. Employed on erecting Nissen Huts on site. Two section in CURLU - Rifle & Squad drill. Gas helmet drill.	O.B.R.
"	" 3		Two sections in MARICOURT erecting Nissen Huts. Two sections proceed from CURLU to MARICOURT with Section transport. Billeted in Nissen Huts. Employed on erecting Nissen Huts for Div. HQ. Co. HQ remain at CURLU.	O.B.R.
"	" 4		4 Sections in MARICOURT erecting Nissen Huts. Reconnoiting district for water supply. Three lime are for Div. HQ. Huts camouflaged & sketching areas nailing acorn. Lt/c. Larkman's coldbuttry struck. Work as on 4th inst. Internal fittings & huts commenced. Major E.W. Ormston R.E. returns from leave.	O.B.R.
"	" 5		Work as on 4th inst.	O.B.R.
"	" 6		Work up to 2 p.m. as on 4th inst. Total work 11 huts complete 3 70% complete. 2 Sections return to billets in CURLU to resume work on MARICOURT- PERONNE Railway. 2 Sections return to billets in CLERY to commence work on new road at CLERY station.	O.B.R.
"	" 7		2 Sections employed in ballasting and draining MARICOURT-PERONNE Rly at B27c. as yds ballasted. 2 Sections employed continually, endrawing approach at CLERY Station. Strength 6 Off. 207 O.R. (including 1 Off. 7 O.R. detached from Coy.) Attached 1 Off. 2 O.R. 1 O.R. admitted to hospital.	O.B.R.
"	" 8		Work as on 7th inst.	
"	" 9		Work as on 7th inst. 1 O.R. joins Coy. from Base.	
"	" 10		Work as on 7th inst.	

WAR DIARY or INTELLIGENCE SUMMARY

Army Form C. 2118

229th FIELD Co R.E.

APRIL 1917

Place	Date	Hour	Summary of Events and Information	Remarks and references to Appendices
CURLU G.6.b.9.4. Map 62c	APRIL 11	—	Orders received by C.O. to move to site new PERONNE bridges. Order cancelled. 2 Sections ordered to move. Section employed on Road construction CLERY. Station move to I 21.6 north of PERONNE. Weather - Fair.	CBR
"	" 12	—	2 Section employed on MARICOURT - PERONNE Railway - Draining - Ballasting. 2 Sections at I.2.b. employed on PERONNE - NURLU Railway (60cm) assembling trackwork. 2 Sections employed on MARICOURT - PERONNE Railway. 3 O.R. join C/o from Base.	CBR
"	" 13	—	Work as on 12th	
"	" 14	—	Work as on 12th. 2 O.R. admitted to Hospital. 1 Offr proceeds on leave. Strength 7 off 210 O.R. (including 2 off & 12 O.R. detached from Coy.) Attached 2 off 12 O.R.	CBR
"	" 15	—	Work as on 14th. Orders received for Coy to take over work in hive till 12th hy Bgds. 2 O.R. admitted to Hospital. Preparations made for moving. 1 O.R. rejoin C/o from Hospital.	CBR
EQUANCOURT V.10.b.3.9. 57c	16		2 Sections at I.2.b. employed on PERONNE - NURLU Railway (60cm) assembling trackwork. C/o Hd Qrs & 2 Sections proceed by motor lorries to EQUANCOURT. Billeted in ruins & houses. Construct billets etc. C.S.M. proceeds on leave U.K. 1 O.R. admitted to Hospital. 1 O.R. rejoin C/o from Hospital.	CBR
"	17		2 Section at PERONNE work as on 16th inst. HQ + 2 Section continuing billets - EQUANCOURT. Bgde Hd.Qrs repaired. Company & Divisional work Battalion personnel attached to Coy for work disciplining sections.	CBR
"	18		2 Section: PERONNE work as on 16th inst. 2 Section employed carrying on main line of Resistance - Q.27.b. Billet improvements. Repairs to Bgde Hd.Qrs. 2 O.R. rejoin C/o from hospital.	CBR

WAR DIARY or INTELLIGENCE SUMMARY

Army Form C. 2118

(3)

229th FIELD COY R.E.   407th DIVISION

APRIL 1917.

Place	Date	Hour	Summary of Events and Information	Remarks and references to Appendices
EQUANCOURT V.10.b.3.9.	APRIL 19th		2 Sections billetted in PERONNE employed in assembling 60 cm trackwork for PERONNE–NURLU Railway. 2 Section in EQUANCOURT employed in construction and improvements of billets & repair of 120 H.Y. Bgde. Hd. Qrs. – EQUANCOURT. 1 Section at V.25.d. Field Cor. R.E. attached for duty. Rev. E. Jones, C.F. detached from C.F. with 19th R.W.F. for duty.	A2R
"	" 20		2 Section on PERONNE–NURLU Railway as on 19th. 3 Section wiring on main line of Resistance Q.21, Q.27, Q.25. Line 'A' Riots wired. Difficulty experienced in getting sufficient material. Captured German barbed wire largely used. Wire C.P. emptied of enemy material. All wiring done at night.	A2R
"	21		2 Section on PERONNE–NURLU Railway as on 19th. 3 Section wiring on main line of Resistance Q.21, 27, 25. Strength per G.S. 7 off. 210 OR (including 2 off 11 OR detached) Attached 3 N. 205 OR.	
"	22		2 Sections on PERONNE–NURLU Railways as on 19th. 1 Section wiring front line at Q.17.a, Q.27.c. 1 Section attached Advanced Brigade Hd Qrs. (Bunker position) for 120 H.Y. Bgde. on Rear Bgte. Hd Qrs. at W.1. b.0.6. cleaning out & deepening well at V.10.b & 7.0 erection of	A2R
"	23		1 Section on PERONNE–NURLU Railway as on 19th but 1 Section wiring on main line of Resistance (at night). 1 Section wiring new Advanced Bgde HdQrs Q.17.c. 2 O.R. from Coy. attached well in EQUANCOURT – erecting Rear Bgte. Hd. Qrs. 2 O.R. detached for duty at XV Corps School.	A2R
"	24		2 Section on PERONNE–NURLU Railway as on 19th but 120 H.Y. Bgde preparing to attach. BEAUCAMP at 4.15 am. 25 Lt. Preparations made for Consolidation. Dumps of tools & wiring material formed at Q.23.b.9.3, Q.17 & 53, Q.29.a.3.3. eros at	

WAR DIARY or INTELLIGENCE SUMMARY

Army Form C. 2118

229 FIELD Cy R.E.

APRIL 1917.

Place	Date	Hour	Summary of Events and Information	Remarks and references to Appendices
EQUANCOURT	APRIL 24		MAP FRANCE Sheet 57c 3 Sections standing by to consolidate if attack succeeds. 1 officer attached to Bgde Hd Qrs as Liaison Officer.	CRE
	25		2 Sections on PERONNE - NURLU Railway as on 19 hr. Exterior of New Bgde Hd Qrs. Attack unsuccessful. No R.E. work until night. 1 Section working on Strong Points at R.7.a.2.9. & at R.14.a.2.8. Completed, garrisoned 1 Section working on strong point at Q.11.d.5.5. Completed hut not wired. Simple Y a + Strong points switched & well wired. Garrison req. 1 platoon. Reconnaissance of wells in VILLERS PLOUICH. Hostile artillery shelled villages & tracks roads on approaches to front line but did not interfere with work on Strong Points. 2 O.R. wounded.	CRE
"	26		1 O.R. admitted to Hospital. 1 O.R. joined Coy from Base. 1 O.R. transferred to 10th Reinforcement Cp. 1 O.R. rejoined coy from Hospital. 2 Sections on PERONNE NURLU Railway as on 19 hr. 3 Section standing by for consolidation work. Dump of wiring material formed at Q.29.a. 1 O.R. attached to Coy from CRE: HdQrs. 1 O.R. rejoins coy from Reserve.	CRE
"	27		2 Section on PERONNE NURLU Railway. 2 Section new hts forward billets in wood at Q.25.a.0.7. Largest amount of wiring material taken forward. New line twixt along white Brigade Front. Seven pickets put in Hostile cable front a 50% wired. 2 O.R admitted to Hospital 1 O.R. rejoins Coy for Coy.	
"	28		2 Section on PERONNE - NURLU Railway. Order received for these to be withdrawn on 29. 3 Sections wiring in Brigade Front.	CRE

WAR DIARY
INTELLIGENCE SUMMARY

229 FIELD COY. RE

APRIL 1917.

Sheet 57 C. ⅛₀,₀₀₀

Place	Date	Hour	Summary of Events and Information	Remarks and references to Appendices
EQUANCOURT	Mr. 29		2 Section rejoin Coy from PERONNE. Billeted in EQUANCOURT. 1 Section of 231st Field Coy RE rejoin 231st F.W.Cy. 2 Section wiring on Byrle front. Laying out Front line Trench from dug to 18" to R7 centre – R7.b.3.0. (700 yds) Trench dug to 15" from Q12.b.02 – Q12.a.23 and Q12.b.32 – Q12.b.54. 1 O.R. from Divisional Gas School for course of instruction.	W.D.
	30		2 Sections move into found billets at Wood Q.2.B. or O.7. Work Coy moves to found billets in same wood. Billeted – Tents, shelters etc. Wiring on Byrle front. Deepen Trenches Card not in 29"	W.D.

O R Rawson
Captn R.E.

MAJOR R.E.
COMMDG. 229th FIELD COMPANY R.E.

CONFIDENTIAL

Vol 12

229th Field Co. R.E.

War Diary

From 1st May 1917
To 31st May 1917

Volume 12

WAR DIARY or INTELLIGENCE SUMMARY

Army Form C. 2118

229th FIELD COY R.E. 40th DIV.

MAY 1917

Place	Date	Hour	Summary of Events and Information	Remarks and references to Appendices
EQUANCOURT	May 1		Work. Wiring on Brigade front. Deepening existing front line trench, laying out and digging further portion of the new trench on brigade front. Coy. H.Q. moved to DESART WOOD W.1.a.9.5. Billeted in huts. No 3 section withdrawn from line for rest. Billeted in EQUANCOURT. 1 O.R. return from leave. 1 O.R. dysentery to hospital.	A.R.
DESART WOOD W.1.a.9.5	2		Work. Wiring on Brigade front. Practically complete. Deepening of trench. Parts of new front line trench No 3 section employed on billet improvements in EQUANCOURT. No 4 section withdrawn from GOUZEAUCOURT to work in DESART WOOD. No 2 section employed on dugouts & well at GOUZEAUCOURT WOOD, making frames for revetting well. Erection of billets in DESART WOOD. 1 O.R. from Corps from leave.	A.R.
"	3		Work. Thickening wire on half Bn. front, front line trench continued. Well — GOUZEAUCOURT WOOD continued. Cupola shelters erected at Bn Battle Head Quarters 17 ft deep. Wire entanglement erected round new Battle H.Q.s. Communication to trench 8" deep & 3'-6" wide. 1 O.R. return from hospital.	A.R.
"	4		Lys Bn H.Q. Wiring round H.Q. completed. Well at GOUZEAUCOURT WOOD continued. Billet improvements in EQUANCOURT continued. Billets in GOUZEAUCOURT WOOD heavily shelled. 1 O.R. wounded. No further damage.	A.R.
"	5		Cupola shelters at 6 ½ 2 S.S. completed. Deepening 1 front line and communication trenches continued Well at GOUZEAUCOURT WOOD continued. Billet improvements at EQUANCOURT continued.	A.R.

WAR DIARY
INTELLIGENCE SUMMARY

Army Form C. 2118

229TH FIELD COY R.E. 40 DIV.

MAY 1917.   MAP. FRANCE Sheet 57c. 1/40,000

Place	Date	Hour	Summary of Events and Information	Remarks and references to Appendices
DESART WOOD W.1.a.9.5.	MAY 5		Billets at GOUZECOURT WOOD treacted. Work Coy return to DESART WOOD. Erection of tents & shelters in DESART WOOD. Coy. standing by - night 5-6 dummy attack on LA VACQUERIE by 40 DIV. Strength 2/12 O.R. including 1 Off — 9 O.R. detached 7 Off 178 O.R. attacked.	CRE
"	6		Work on front line and communication trenches resumed on night 6-7. Wire on Front thickened in parts. Well at GOUZECOURT W05 continued. Billets - EQUANCOURT continued. Night of 6/7 was unusually quiet - no artillery retaliation, very little rifle or M.G. Enemy fired a large number of Red and Green lights about 3.0 a.m.	CRE
"	7		Work on front line Communication trenches continued - deepening and extending. Erection of new battle H.Q. Well at GOUZECOURT WOOD continued. Improvement of Billets - EQUANCOURT.	CRE
"	8		Work as on 7th. Work on second line of defence continued. Trenches laid out. Existing wiring in Brigade front continued.	CRE
"	9		Work as on 8th.	
"	10		Work as on 8th.	
"	11		Work as on 8th. Orders received that Coy. is to be relieved by 23rd Field Coy. & to proceed on 12th to HEUDICOURT to take over line in front of GONNELIEU.	CRE
HEUDICOURT W.21.a.2.1.	12		Work on old sector finished over to 23rd Field Co. R.E. Company less Transport & M.H. personnel proceed to HEUDICOURT & took over from 15" Field Co. R.E. Officers take over work in line. Company improving + extending billets etc	CRE
"	13		Transport & Mtd. personnel proceed to HEUDICOURT. Coy. employed on GREEN LINE (second line of defence) wiring and extending wired system on left of & side of communication trenches front	CRE

Army Form C. 2118

WAR DIARY
or
INTELLIGENCE SUMMARY

(Erase heading not required.) 229 Field Co. R.E. 40° Division

MAY 1917.

Place	Date	Hour	Summary of Events and Information	Remarks and references to Appendices
HEUDICOURT W.4.a.2.1.	MAY 13		Map 57c 1/40,000 Strength: 7 Off. 211 O.R. (Including 1 N/4 & 2 O.R. detached) Attached 2 ff. 175 O.R.	O.B.R.
"	14		Wiring and extending trench system on GREEN LINE. Thick wire erected. Party five trench days. Communication trenches deepened.	O.B.R.
"	15		Wiring on Green Line in R.32.a. Continuing deepening and extending left flank of GREEN LINE. Wiring on front line. Deepening trenches and connecting isolated trenches in SUPPORT LINE. Repair on FINS Rd near HEUDICOURT. Constructing roads to maintain watering point. 3 wells in freely watering water. Wells in GONNELIEU repaired. Work on 15" hut. Heavy rain all night and extreme darkness rendered work almost impossible.	O.B.R.
"	16.		Wiring on GREEN LINE in R31 a 2b. continued. Thick belt fixing being put in. Drainage of front line undertaken work started on Ryr. water main & water were puddle, trump holes put in where other methods is impossible. New position of first Eng tread sited exp't looked. 1 O.R. joins from base.	O.B.R.
"	17		1 O.R. returned from leave to U.K.	O.B.R.
"	18		Wiring on Green line. Wiring of communication trench from Support line forwards. Siting of Communication trench for Suffolk Ho. Trench puck dug. Improvement of Brigade Hd. Qrs. Front Line. Extending of fire trench.	O.B.R.

1875 Wt. W593/826 1,000,000 4/15 J.B.C. & A. A.D.S.S./Forms/C. 2118.

WAR DIARY
INTELLIGENCE SUMMARY

(Erase heading not required.)

Army Form C. 2118

229th Field Coy R.E. 40th Div.

MAY 1917.

Place	Date	Hour	Summary of Events and Information	Remarks and references to Appendices
HEUDICOURT	MAY 19		Coy. employed wiring on Green line. Diggs. communication trench forward from Support line on left. Entering the trench - front line. Two strong points on site East of GONNELIEU sited. Strong points to cover fronts of Village sited. Left of M.G. fire along wire. M.G. Emplacements put in Heavy Cover out. Improvement of Bugle hd.Qrs. Stokes Gun Emplacement sited commenced. Open Stokes Gun Emplacement water construction. Work as on 19.	CRE
	20		Strength: 7 Off. 212 men included 1 off & 8 on detached. Attached 2 off. 182 —	CRE
	21		Machine Gun Emplacement in Strong Point S of GONNELIEU constructed. Work as on 19 also wiring of Reserve Line on left. 1 off Cattacked infantry & 1 off admitted to hospital. Open Stokes Gun Emplacement completed.	CRE
	22		Work as on 19. Wiring on front line continued. Sup Trench - front line :- Reserve line deepened. New trench dug. Communication trenches deepened & extended forwards. Water point on FINS ROAD Carried forward. 1 O.R. proceeds to U.K. on leave.	CRE
	23		1 O.R. admitted to hospital.	CRE
	24		Company employed in line & in left work line, Support & reserve line - front trench. Spitlocked, very little revetment from Support line. Cambrelin stairs dug for Stokes Gun crews, wiring extension of accommodation for Reserve Battle. 1 O.R. admitted to hospital. 1 O.R. proceeds U.K. on leave	CRE

WAR DIARY
INTELLIGENCE SUMMARY

Army Form C. 2118

(Erase heading not required.) 229 Field C.F.E. A.O"D.

MAY. 1917.

Place	Date	Hour	Summary of Events and Information	Remarks and references to Appendices
HEUDICOURT	MAY 25		MAP. FRANCE. Sheet 57 c. 1/40.000. Trench work carried on during night. Shotlocking Switch kept between front & support lines. Work continued on Reserve Line. 2 C.'s of Pioneers supplied for the work. 1 Section resting. 2 O.R. admitted to hospital.	O.B.R.
"	26		Work as night of 25th sector handed over to 204 Field Co. 36th Div. Work on new after relief & new sector was reorganized. New front extends R.34.a. to R.20.b. Orders received at 4.0 p.m. to move C.O. to DESSART WOOD. Fwd Section, H.Q.'s & attached works C.A. proceed to DESSART WOOD accommodated in Eng. shelters. Transport Camp stores moved to SORREL LE GRAND. V.24.b.35.55. 1 O.R. admitted to hospital.	O.B.R.
DESSART WOOD W.1.a.9.5.	27		Construction of Cub. & Cover Shelters &c in Reserve Line. Extension of Reserve Line on Right. 2 C.'s of Pioneers working on the Strong Point at QUENTIN MILL R.31.d. commenced. Wiring of Switch line behind Front line has been Strength 7 Off. 211 men including 1 Off. 12 m detached. March 1 Off. — 179 — 1 O.R. admitted to hospital.	O.B.R.
"	28		Cub. & Cover Shelters continued. Strong Point continued. Wire obstacle laid & further Reassurance for Watercarts made forward GONNELIEU.	
"	29		Work as on 28. 1 Officer joined Coy from leave 2nd Lieut. G.F. DURSTON R.E. as Supernumerary Officer. 1 Officer proceed on leave to U.K.	
"	30			
"	31		Work as on 25 continued. O.C. on forward situ over eighth HINDENBURG Line commencing at GONNELIEU. Pat New Front Line loped out. This line lies in front of the main front line & is a reserve slope sit. New front line: Construction of welle from GONNELIEU GRUER Capt R.E.	U.B.R.

MAJOR R.E.
MNOR. 229th FIELD COMPANY R.E.

Confidential

WAR DIARY

229 Field Coy. R.E.

VOLUME I

JUNE 1917.

WAR DIARY or INTELLIGENCE SUMMARY

Army Form C. 2118

229th Field Co RE. 40th Division

MAP. FRANCE. SHEET 57 c /40,000. JUNE 1917.

Place	Date	Hour	Summary of Events and Information	Remarks and references to Appendices
DESSART WOOD W.1.a.9.5.	June 1st		Head Quarters and Two Sections and attached Company of Infantry billeted in DESSART WOOD. Two Sections working in line billeted in huts & in shelters near railway siding at GOUZEAUCOURT. Transport at SORREL-le-GRAND. Company working in GOUNELIEU sector. General trench work, drainage of existing trenches. Strongthening of two main communication trenches No's 3 Village & No 4 Observation line. Strengthen Point Contracto & Strong Points at R.31.a.12. Constructn of artillery O.P in GOUNELIEU	OBR
	2		Work in line as on 1st. Clearing well in GOUNELIEU for establishment of water point. Strength 8 off. 208 o.r. inclusive.	CBR
	3		Attached 1 off. 7 or detached. 1 off. 3 or on leave. Major EVORMSTON RE awarded D.S.O.	CBR
	4		Work in line as on 2nd. Infantry. 179 o.r. 1/Cst QUEBDITS extracted. Enemy mine removed from cellar house – GOUZEAUCOURT – GOUVEAUCOURT heavily shelled neighborhood of forward billets 1 O.R. wounded.	OBR
	5		Work in line as on 2nd. to Golden Rain. Rockets sent up by Enemy. Mistaken by our East battalion in line as signal to open trench mortar fire on enemy. Scheme of Brigade altered to field comm. 1 Or funeral company.	OT
	6		Work in line as on 2nd. New Front line dug to 5' depth in material wire front communicath trenches up to New line deepened. 2 O.R. proceed on leave	CBR
	7		Work as on 5. 1 O.R. rejoined company from hospital. Major LAKE R.A.M.C. attached to company for instruction.	OBR

1875. Wt. W593/826 1,000,000 4/15 J.B.C. & A. A.D.S.S./Forms/C.2118.

WAR DIARY

229th FIELD Cy R.E. 46th DIVISION

JUNE 1917

NAP: FRANCE. Sheet 57c / A.O.7000

Place	Date	Hour	Summary of Events and Information	Remarks and references to Appendices
—	7		Gas alarm sounded about 11.0 pm. Agen Wood to Enemy "Golden rain" rockets. 1 O.R. proceeds on leave.	OBR
—	8		Work in Engr. room 5.	
—	9		Work in hut on 5. Reconnaissance of GOUZEAUCOURT - CAMBRAI ROAD made up to No man's land with view to wiring, trees & junctions & filling shell holes etc. Officer proceeds on leave. Strength Effective, 8 Off. 209 OR including 1 W. - 7 OR detached and 1 W. - 7 OR on leave	OBR
—	10		Attached 3 M 224 OR 2 of major company from leave. Work in Engr. as a 5. Also Buckram wire in front of new front line. Laying of drains for communication trench S. of Gonnelieu. 2 LT HUDSON RE transferred for duty with Divisional Works. 1 OR admitted hospital.	OBR
—	11		Work as on 10. New wagon road up to left bank. Four opened up (level cross?). 1 Off returned from leave. Major Evans RE + 1 Off from 238 A.T. Cy, R.E. attached	OBR
—	12		Work as on 10. 1 hund kidg. on new wagon road. Wiring party of 48 Infantry from Battalion on relief. 1 20. N. Byles is Evac. to 121 Vfield Ambl. 1 Off attached to C.R.E. & O/C H.Qrs. Major LAKE A.D.C. leaves Cy. is attached "RCFE" HQ. 2 of formerly transferred to Centr - Schol.	OBR
—	13		Work us on 10 in Engr. Major Evans RE O.C. 238 AT CyRE take command of company. Major F.W. ORMISTON RE leaves Cy & takes command of 238 AT Cy RE for one month. 1 OR granted leave to UK. 1 admittes to hospital	OBR

WAR DIARY or INTELLIGENCE SUMMARY

229 Field Coy R.E. A.O. 2w

Place	Date	Hour	Summary of Events and Information	Remarks and references to Appendices
DESSART WOOD N.19.a.95	JUNE 14		MAP FRANCE 57° D/SOOO	
	June 15		Work as on 15th. Evacuation of New Front Line Trench pushed on.	ORR
	" 16		Work as on 14.	ORR
			Coy Strength 7 off. 216 OR. motors. 14 off 71 nco attached and Lt/Lt 6 on leave.	
			Attached. 3 off. 151 OR.	
	" 17		1 OR granted leave. 2 OR return from leave.	ORR
			R/E. dump formed at R.20.d.5.A. at forward end drew 2. OR. sum avg from Base. 3 OR. return from leave. 1 OR. regains enr for ASC.	
	" 18		Work as on 14. New RE dump formed under bank on road at GOUZEAUCOURT-CANAL R.26.d.95.80. Forward dumps at head of Sap wiring supplies wire + Pickets - for wiring supplies need doing. 2 OR. attached to hospital. 1 OR. proceeds U.K. on leave.	ORR
	" 19		Work as on 18. towards dumps at Sap heads increased. 1 OR granted leave.	ORR
	" 20		General trench work in Brigade front. Constructing Company Station = GOUZEAUCOURT. Wiring front of new front line trench. 1 OR. returns from leave. 1 OR. to hospital.	ORR
	21		General trench work in brigade front. 1 OR to Field Hospital.	ORR

WAR DIARY or INTELLIGENCE SUMMARY

Army Form C. 2118 (A)

229 Field Coy R.E. 40 Div

Place	Date	Hour	Summary of Events and Information	Remarks and references to Appendices
DESSART WOOD N1a 9/5	June 22		Map France 57c  1/40,000. General trench work, front sympathies with Dimmis on Riget (S5). Trench sites & new front line to be constructed on Roger Scaff. Taped out and posts marked out. Chief point alone new line scheme: to wire whole frontage the first night (23 night) and dig the posts out. The posts to be held. Engineers to put = the wire, helps the infantry to which were gradually and extend posts to meet on flanks – so from a line. 1 OR to hospital. 1 OR on leave.	CRE
	23		General trench work. Line formed on Right Bn front put out. No interference from the enemy except at one point where a group rapid fire & went fires by M.G. 1 OR wounded. Strength 7 Off. 206 OR inclusion 2 off + 13 m.o. detached (1 off + 5 OR on leave) Attached 3 Off. 120 O.R.	CRE
—	24		General trench work. Trench mortar emplacements near GONNELIEU continued from Beaux. 1 OR joined Coy.	
—	25		General Trench work. Communication trenches to new posts in new front line continued. New line of wire young put in front of posts. 1 OR Evacuated to Base Depot. which time was too close. 2 OR proceed on leave. 1 OR rejoin from hospital. Part Full SCRE for work in Div. Pi. Dump. 1 OR attached	CRE
—	26		General Trench work. Cutting trees in CANGRAI Rgd and finishing. 1 OR rejoin from leave. 1 OR proceed to Hospital. 1 off + 2 OR attaches to Army Infantry School for instruction	

WAR DIARY

INTELLIGENCE SUMMARY

June 1917. 228 Field Coy R.E.

Place	Date	Hour	Summary of Events and Information	Remarks and references to Appendices
DESSART WOOD W.1.a.9.5	Jun 27	5° /40000	General Trench work. Spittacks new Communication Trench to new Posts. Efforts made to get all part Spate of Trench boarded (run up). 1 O.R. proceed on leave. 1 O.R. A.S.C. 2 O.R. Div. Employment C° attached.	4SR
	" 28		General Trenchwork. 1 O.R. proceed to School of Instruction at ABBEYVILLE. 1 O.R. set to England to report to SPRS Chatham for instruction in Cable Laying.	SR
	" 29		General Trench work. 2 O.R. proceed on leave.	
	30		Do. Strength 7 off, 203 O.R. including 3 off, 24 O.R. attached (1 off, 13 O.R. leave) Attached 2 off, 16 O.R.	CSR

OBRaymond
MAJOR R.E.
228th FIELD COMPANY R.E.

— CONFIDENTIAL —

Vol 14

WAR DIARY.

OF

229th FIELD COMPANY. R.E.

VOLUME 14

JULY, 1917.

WAR DIARY or INTELLIGENCE SUMMARY

Army Form C. 2118

229th FIELD Coy RE. 40th Div.

July 1917

MAP. FRANCE Sheet 57c 1/40,000.

Place	Date	Hour	Summary of Events and Information	Remarks and references to Appendices
DESSART WOOD W.1.a.9.5.	July 1st		Company employed on general trench work in GONNELIEU sector, also construction & carpentry in new front line, manufacture of Bangalore Torpedoes for use of Infantry on Raids, construction of water point — GONNELIEU (well being cleaned out) 2 OR attached from 353 Coy M.G.C to drive Bore holes for water. 1 OR rejoined from Hospital. 1 OR proceed on leave. 3 OR from leave.	ORR
	2nd		Work in line as 1st. Cutting of trees in CAMBRAI Rd. 2 OR proceed on leave. 1 OR from leave. Repair of Roads continued.	ORR
	3rd		Work in line as 1st. 2 OR proceed on leave. 1 OR from leave.	ORR
	4th		Work in line as 1st. 1 OR proceed on leave.	ORR
	5th		Work in line as 1st. 3 OR proceed on leave.	ORR
	6th		Work in line as 1st. 1 OR killed, 2 OR wounded (attached infantry) 1 OR from leave. Pd mag cap which exploded.	ORR
	7		Major EVANS 1 OR returns from leave. Major E.W. ORMISTON RE resumes command of company. Work in line as 1st to 229 (A.T.) Coy RE. 1 OR from leave. 1 OR on leave. 1 OR to Hospital. 3 OR proceed on leave. Construction of Baths attended in GOUZEAUCOURT. Strength Effective 7 off. 203 OR including 1 off. 26 OR attached. (1 OR on leave) Attached 1 off. 14 g OR.	ORR
	8.		Work in line as 1st.	ORR
SUNKEN ROAD W.9.d.8.7.	9.		Work in line as 1st. Coy H.Q. 2 Sections and works Coys moved from DESSART WOOD and proceed to Sunken Rd. W.9.d.8.7. Consolidated & shelter tents. to reduce distance between H.Q. & work in line. More cannot cut.	ORR

WAR DIARY
or
INTELLIGENCE SUMMARY

229TH FIELD COY.R.E. 40TH DIV.

Army Form C. 2118

Place	Date	Hour	Summary of Events and Information	Remarks and references to Appendices
SUNKEN ROAD M9.d.8.y.	July 10		MAP FRANCE Sht. 57 C. 1/20,000. General Trench work = GONNELIEU SECTOR. Water Point = GOUZEAUCOURT - GONNELIEU were constructed. Bout at GOUZEAUCOURT or also Bore Hole for water supply continued. Cutting of Trees on CAMBRAI ROAD continued. 1 OR return C.T from Base.	O.R.
	" 11		General Trench work as on 10". Raid attempted by party of Riflemen on Emergency Trip. Dis Loyella Failed (4" drug platform) 2 OR. attacks to 4 Army School of Sanitation Reg A. OR. join CT from Base. 1 OR return from leave.	O.R.
	" 12		General Trench work	O.R.
	13		General Trench work. 1 OR. killed 3 OR. wounded in action by Trench Mortar Fire.	O.R.
	" 14		General Trench work. New front line continued. Sand Bag Barricade across road at R27. a. 4.4. trophic house completed in C.T. R27 a X6. Road at R31 b-5 camouflaged. Strength of Company. Tot. 207 OR. incls 1 off 12 OR detailed on duty 13 OR on leave attached Infantry 24 - 162 OR.	O.R.
	15		General Trenchwork. 1 OR attached to School of Sanitation for Instruction. 2 OR. rejoin from School Sanitation.	O.R.
	16.		General Trench work. Work on Articles of: Wells. Camouflage from Barricade, etc. 3 OR. rejoin from leave. 1 OR. join CT from Base.	O.R.

WAR DIARY or INTELLIGENCE SUMMARY

Army Form C. 2118

229th FIELD Coy R.E. 40th DIVISION

JULY 1917.

Place	Date	Hour	Summary of Events and Information	Remarks and references to Appendices
SUNKEN ROAD W.9.d.8.7.	July 17.		MAP FRANCE 57C 1/40,000. General trench work and work as on 16. New Cuklellen OP started. To be constructed by R.7 & 3 PLATES a Mine Crater. 1 Officer (Lieut. G. DURSTON, R.E.) wounded on active service on duty. 3 O.R. rejoin from leave. 3 O.R. join from base. 1 O.R. to Hospital.	O.R.R.
	18.		Trench work etc, as above. Construction of Splinter Proof Shelters - Front line Support & Reserve continued. Trench boarding of "C.T.'s" & Support Head. 1 O.R. rejoins from 51st M.VS. 2 O.R. rejoin from leave.	O.R.R.
	19.		Trench work etc as on 18. 1 O.R. rejoin from leave. 1 O.R. wounded in action.	O.R.R.
	20.		General Trench work. Deepening of "C.T." to new Fire Trench & deepening & extending of F.T. continued. Work commenced & work maintenance between GOUZEAUCOURT & GONNELIEU & main transport road. 1 O.R. proceeds on leave. 1 O.R. to Hospital.	O.R.R.
	21.		General Trench work etc. 1 O.R. rejoins from 231st Field Coy. R.E. (for attachment to M.O. staff.) 1 O.R. rejoins from School of Sanitation. 2 O.R. from leave. 2 O.R. proceed to A1 1st Stationary Hospital for rest. 1 O.R. rejoins from Hospital. Strength 7 Off 259 O.R. 1 Off 15 men attached in leave. Artillery Strength 2 Off 163 O.R. unit & 1 Off 15 men attached in leave.	O.R.R.
	22.		General Trench work. Wiring of Artillery positions by CAMBRAI Rd. One section resting.	O.R.R.
	23.		General Trench work etc. Construction of Divisional BnHQ. HQ continued. 1 O.R. to Hospital.	O.R.R.
	24.		General Trench work & Special work as above. 2 O.R. to Hospital.	O.R.R.
	25.		General Trench work etc. Erection of Shelters at Newton's Post (advanced position) begun, & Trench Boards in C.T.'s. 1 O.R. to Hospital.	O.R.R.
	26.		Work as on 24.	

WAR DIARY or INTELLIGENCE SUMMARY

Army Form C. 2118

229th FIELD COY R.E. 40th DIV.

July 1917.

Place	Date	Hour	Summary of Events and Information	Remarks and references to Appendices
SUNKEN ROAD W.9.d.5.7.	July 27		General Trenchwork as above. Drainage of trenches continued. New line of wire on the North of GONNELIEU Expedient.	
"	28		General Trenchwork. Strength Officers 7 OR – 208 OR including 2 Off – 150 OR detached + 1 OR Leave. A32.	
	29		General Trenchwork. 10 OR reserves from forward.	O32. Civis Euro
	30		ditto	
	31		ditto	

EwMM
Major RE
OC 229 F Coy RE

Confidential

War Diary of 229th Field Company R.E.

From 1st August 1917
to 31st August 1917

WAR DIARY or INTELLIGENCE SUMMARY
(Erase heading not required.)

Army Form C. 2118

229th FIELD Coy. R.E. A.O. DIVISION

MAP: FRANCE Sheet 57c / 40,000.

Month and Year: AUGUST 1917

Place	Date	Hour	Summary of Events and Information	Remarks and references to Appendices
SUNKEN ROAD W.9.d.8.7.	Aug 1st		General Trench work in GONNELIEU SECTOR. Excavation of new front line to depth almost completed, drainage French Revetting, firestepping, etc. carried on also C.T. T.M. Emplacements, shelters & front line etc. of mule evacuation at back of GONNELIEU. Water supply scheme continued. Motor pump installed. 1 O.R. gone from heart.	A.R.
	Night 1/ Aug 1/2		Raid on enemy's trench in R.20.c. organised by line Battn. Party of Sappers at three points with Bangalore to take enemy wire & mobile charges to blow in dug-outs. Gap successfully blown by Bangalore & party went through to trench. Suffers wire first & its trench - threaded away front line to Communication Trench. As enemy was returned to trench, these (?) were blown in - also part of front line. Party would repair dug-outs. Enemy's front line found to be about 6'0" deep & 3'6" broad & not firestepped. Lieut. W.G. ROBB R.E. wounded by M.G. but 3 O.R. wounded.	C.B.R.
	2.		General Trench work. Division side slips work with Lieut. 1 Bunker frontage. BOMB howitzer over from 231st Field Coy. R.E. Trenches in very wet condition shallow and water to 229 had to go R.E. first Camp not done wire very very thin New Battn just on left in VILLERS-PLOUICH SECTOR. River Banks too exposed from R.1.4.b. 67.b. R.27. d. 52. Ripper Bridge	
	3.		General Trench work as of 1st	
	4.		General Trench work Ripper. Battn relief on left preventing work. from 4 Army Infantry detail.	C.R.R
			Strength 6 Off. 205 O.R. males 2/ 1 off - 13 O.R. detached. Att 1 off. 1 W.O. 2 off. repn empld. 1 O.R. proceeds to "N." C.C.S. inf arty 2 off. 157 O.R.	C.R.R.
			Work on left commenced. Gap = front line trench cleared & trench dug 4'3" x 3'0" & repaired on flank.	
	5.		General Trench work. Front had on left deepened + wire = first finished. 1 O.R. report to hospital.	C.R.R.

WAR DIARY or INTELLIGENCE SUMMARY

229th FIELD Coy. R.E. 40th DIVISION.

AUGUST 1917.

MAP: FRANCE Sheet 57C/10000.

Place	Date	Hour	Summary of Events and Information	Remarks and references to Appendices
SUNKEN ROAD W.9.d.8.7.	Aug. 6		General Trench Work. Wire in left flank needed & new belt in front commenced. Infantry made great improvements to trench by digging out the mud, employing reliefs etc. A very little labour was required.	
	7		1 O.R. returns from hospital.	
	7		Camp in Bush area started. Cook for Bath (Standing Dept) (to be erected), Nissen huts, Kitchen Cookhouse latrines etc. 1 sector surveyed on the work.	
	8		General Trench Work. Cpl. Winter Smyth & Ramp erection no advance. 1 O.R. granted leave.	O.R.R.
	9		General Trench work as on 7. M.O. Div. R.E. + 3 O.R. attached to Company. 2 O.R. for Hospital.	O.S.R.
			Work on an 8" Road repair between GOUZEAUCOURT, GONNELIEU continues. Road at W.9.d.8.7. taken over by Corps. — work started in its by Company.	O.R.
	10		General Trench work as on 9th. Work on Camp water supply Road approach (CONNELIEU-GOUZEACOURT) go on. 9 = 1 O.R. att Third Army School of Cookery. 2/Lt. P.T. EASTON joined Company from Base.	O.R.O.
	11		Work as on 10th Strength 7 Off. 208 O.R. including 1 Off. + 13 O.R. detached attached 3 Off. 155 O.R.	O.R.O.
	12		General French work to wire thickened on left	O.R.O.
			1 O.R. granted leave. 2/Lieut DURSTON classified "wounded" shell shock W" by D.A.G. 3rd Echelon.	O.R.O.
	13		Work as on 12th	O.R.O.
	14		General French Work to 1 O.R. granted leave.	O.R.O.

WAR DIARY or INTELLIGENCE SUMMARY

Army Form C. 2118

229th Field Coy. R.E. 40th Division

(3)

MAP: FRANCE Sheet 57d SE 1/40000

Place	Date	Hour	Summary of Events and Information	Remarks and references to Appendices
SUNKEN ROAD W.9.d.8.9.	Aug 15		Work as on 14th. Repairing Baths in COUZEAUCOURT. Filling Mine Craters at Q.36.C.5.0.	Nil
	16		1 O.R. to hospital	Nil
	17		General Trench work to as on 15th	Nil
	18		General Trench work to as on 14th. CAPTAIN A.B. RAYNER granted leave	
	19		General Trench work to as on 16th. 1 O.R. granted leave. Strength 6 Off. 207 O.R. including 1 O.R. detached 1 O.R. rejoined from hospital. 1 Off. 5 O.R. on leave. Attached Sept/54 1 O.R. on duty.	Nil
	20		General trench work as on 18th. 1 O.R. rejoined from Third Army School of Cookery. 1 O.R. to hospital. 1 O.R. rejoined from leave. 4 O.R. joined Coy from 8th Reinforcement Coy R.E.	Nil
	21		General Trench work as on 20th. 1 O.R. rejoined from leave	Nil
	22		No 1 & 4 Sections at Huts near GOUZEAUCOURT relieved by No 2 & 3 Sections from W.9.d.8.9. No 1 & 4 Sections take over work of No 2 & 3 Sectns 1 O.R. from hospital. 1 O.R. admitted to hospital	Nil
	23		General Trench work. Work commenced on erection of shelters for Volunteers. Work on Dumps to continued	Nil
	24		Work as on 23rd. 2 O.R. joined Coy from 2nd Reinforcement R.E.	Nil

WAR DIARY or INTELLIGENCE SUMMARY

Army Form C. 2118

229th Field Coy R.E. 40th Division (4)

MAP. FRANCE SHEET 57c 1/40000

Place	Date	Hour	Summary of Events and Information	Remarks and references to Appendices
SUNKEN ROAD W.9.d.8.9.	Aug 25		Work as on 24th. Strength 6 Off. 213 O.R. including 10 O.R. detached on duty. 1 Off. 3 O.R. on leave. Attached 3 Off. 152 O.R.	P.T.O.
	26		Bridging posts. General Drench work to as on 25th. 1 O.R. returned from leave. 2 O.R. granted leave. 1 O.R. attached rejoined 40th Divn. A.S.C.	P.T.O.
	27		Work as on 26th. 3 O.R. granted leave. 2/Lieut C.R. BENNETT R.E. joined Coy from Base.	P.T.O.
	28		Work as on 27th. Raid on enemy's trenches by Rear Batt. Dug out blown in whilst Bangalore Torpedo used by party of Sappers. 1 dug out destroyed by mobile charge. Wounded LIEUT R.L. ROLFE R.E. + 1 O.R. 2 O.R. (attached) rejoined 353 T & M Coy R.E.	P.T.O.
	29		Work as on 28th. 2/Lieut A.F. DURSTON R.E. rejoined Coy from hospital. 1 O.R. rejoined from leave. 1 O.R. rejoined from School of Farriers Abbeville	P.T.O.
	30		General Trench work to as on 29th. Raid on enemy trenches by Left Batt. 1 Off. 2/Lieut E.T. BORRIE R.E. + 2 Sappers detailed to blow gap in enemy wire but owing to thickness of wire & bangalore torpedoes being of insufficient length they were unable to do so. Party returned safely to our lines	P.T.O.
	31		General Trench work to as on 30th. 2 O.R. joined Coy from Base.	P.T.O.

E.W. Smith
MAJOR R.E.
O/c 229th FIELD COMPANY R.E.

Vol /6

"Confidential"

WAR DIARY

229th Field Company, Royal Engineers

SEPTEMBER '17

Vol I

Army Form C. 2118.

WAR DIARY
or
INTELLIGENCE SUMMARY.

(Erase heading not required.) 229 FIELD Coy. R.E. 40TH DIVISION

SEPTEMBER 1917

Place	Date	Hour	Summary of Events and Information	Remarks and references to Appendices
SUNKEN ROAD W.9.d.8.7.	SEPT. 1		MAP FRANCE Sheet 57c/40,000. Company in GOUZEAUCOURT Section working with 119th Inf Bde. Employed in general trench work, maintenance & repairs, construction of shelters in front line, excavation of new front line in front of VILLERS PLOUICH, Trench Mortar Emplacements etc. Construction of accommodation for Support and Reserve Battalions for winter, also Winter Camps in HEUDICOURT. Construct of Baths for troops in GOUZEAUCOURT. Water Supply to Support line - GONNELIEU Sector. Construction of Light Railway for Heavy T.M. Ammunition. Repairs of Roads in area. 1 Off. 1 OR rejoin from Court. 1 OR from hospital. Effective Strength Units 7 offs 213 OR including 8 OR detached, 14 - 8 OR on leave Attached M/gators M.O. 3 offs 145 OR	O.R.
	2.		General R.E. work as on 1st. 1 OR attached 4 PERONNE Dental Centre	
	3.		General work as on 1st	9.32
	4.		General work as on 1st	
	5.		General work as on 1st	
	6.		General work as on 1st. 1 OR wounded by direct hit - on right shoulder - End	a/32
	7.		General work as on 1st. Drainage of Trenches. 1 OR blinded. 1 OR from hospital. Pnr. COPLEY awarded Military Medal for gallantry.	9.32 O.R.
	8.		General RE work continued as previous. no new work of importance undertaken. 2 OR rejoin from leave 1 OR granted leave 2 OR to G. Enforce. Effective Strength of Unit 7 offs 213 OR including 9 OR detached 2 8 OR on leave Attached M/gators M.O. 3 offs 139 OR	O.R.

2353 Wt. W2511/1454 700,000 5/15 D.D.&L. A.D.S.S./Forms/C.2118.

Army Form C. 2118.

WAR DIARY
or
INTELLIGENCE SUMMARY.
(Erase heading not required.) 229 FIELD Co RE 40TH DIV (2)

SEPTEMBER 1917.

Place	Date	Hour	Summary of Events and Information	Remarks and references to Appendices
			MAP FRANCE Sheet 57C. 1/40,000	
SUNKEN ROAD. W.9.d.8.7.	Sept. 9		General Trench work in line. Winter accommodation, Roads Water Supply etc. in hand behind the line. 1 OR rejoined fr Pierremont Dental Clinic 1 OR attached to 3rd Army School of Sanitation for instruction in Sanitary duties	CRR
	" 10		Water main to Co HQ or Right completed Revetting in line commenced at R side & continued outwards near "A" frames and Expanded Metal New Strong Point C19 on Right commenced	
	" 11		General work as above. 3 OR from Coast 1 OR granted leave	CRR
	" 12		General work as above. 2 OR Reinf Corps	CRR
	" 13		" " " 1 OR hospital. 1 OR rejoined fr School of Sanitation	CRR
	" 14		" " " 1 OR for hospital 1 OR granted leave Bangalore Torpedo trials carried out in rear. Many can not touch on Enemy trenches General Trench work a/s	CRR
			On the side of CAMBRAI ROAD Parties of Sappers proceeded with Bangalore Torpedoes to cut wire & further accompanying Infantry with Mobile Charges & Blow up Dugouts 1 OR wounded. 2 OR wounded. Excellent plans of dugout fm in construction of Gunn Bogs - OR sliger District from Sgt Kitchen Started 3 partnershipP	CRR
	" 15		General work as above. Major EW. RAYTON to hospital	CRR
	" 16		Effective Strength of Unit: 6 off 211 OR including 13 OR detached at learn Attached to Infantry 1 MO, 3 SB, 1 OR clerk, 5 OR to 3rd Army Rest Camp	CRR CRR CRR
	" 17		General work as above. 1 OR from hospital 1 OR to hospital	
	" 18		" " " Survey of area for Strong Points taken in hand	CRR

WAR DIARY
or
INTELLIGENCE SUMMARY

Army Form C. 2118.

(Erase heading not required.) 229th FIELD Cᵒ RE 40th DIV.

SEPTEMBER 1917.

Place	Date	Hour	Summary of Events and Information	Remarks and references to Appendices
SUNKEN ROAD W.9.d.8.1	Sep 19		MAP FRANCE Sheet 57 C 1/40,000. General RE work i line. Work i rear in Reconstruction, Gun Bns & Cos water supply, Road repairs etc.	CIX CCII OBL
	20		Work as on 19.	
	21		— at — 1 OR on leave. Lieut JG VOCE R.E. from met for Boat.	
	22		Effective Strength Unit: 7 off. 212 OR including 1 off 16 OR detached to 3 OR Coat. Attached to F.A. 3 off 138 OR	
	23		Work i line as name. Reconnaissance made of Barracks + ground near VACQUERIE to fix sites for canal mines to be blown in connection with diversion attacks and relief by Right Brigade. 1 OR on leave. 1 OR attached to 3 Corps Rest Station. Work i line as usual. MAJOR E.W. ORMSTON rejoins from Hospital. Capt F.W. CLARK R.E. to No 231st FIELD Cᵒ R.E. Major ORMSTON assumes command. In evening a party of sappers with infantry patrol to Congés Canal mines i No mans Land and at Barracks. R.1.d.65.45 & R.21.d.O.4. Enfilade.	CIR GSD
	24			
	25		Work i line started as usual. Operation front cut during afternoon completed. Terminal leads to terminal mines laid during day from the cut. Enemy end been stolen. Wires where leads went taken to land mines called up to be blown as zero approached before dark. Enemy opened a front line 2 minutes before zero of attack. 1 OR for Hospital	GSD

WAR DIARY or INTELLIGENCE SUMMARY

Army Form C. 2118.

229 FIELD Co RE 40th Div

Title pages SEPTEMBER 1917

MAP FRENCH Sheet 57C /40,000

Place	Date	Hour	Summary of Events and Information	Remarks and references to Appendices
SUNKEN ROAD Nyd 81	Sept. 26.		Work = Eng as usual	CRE
	" 27.		Work = Eng as usual. 1 off + 2 OR proceed to 53 Corps Rest Station. Work 2 NCO's + 9 Sappers went 2 Bangalore Torpedoes blew gap in wire in South of CAMBRAI ROAD. Sent out with Infantry Patrol to repair after attack. Suffered to retire after enemy gap. Party was seen to by enemy who pursued to Barracks + enemy camp + Rifle, M.G. + Rifle Grenade & Bombs, our wire fires put to get Torpedoes into position. Party had to retire. 5 OR return from 3 Army Rest Camp.	CRE
	28		Work = Eng as usual. 1 OR from leave.	CRE
	29.		Work = Eng as usual. Attempts made to salvo to ca. 9 mins for ar at m 29. The hour was too bright to effect this work. 1 off & OR detail & leave Effective Strength of Unit 7 off. 209 OR.	CRE
	30		Work = Eng as usual.	CRE

A.B.Clayton. Capt. R.E.
O.C. 229 Field Co R.E.

SECRET

WAR DIARY.
229th FIELD Co., R.E.

OCTOBER 1917.

Vol 17

WAR DIARY or INTELLIGENCE SUMMARY

Army Form C. 2118.

229th Field Coy R.E. 40th Division

MAP: France Sheet 57c / 40,000

OCTOBER 1917

Place	Date	Hour	Summary of Events and Information	Remarks and references to Appendices
SONNEN ROAD W.9.d.8.7.	Oct 1st		**Sector** Company attached to 119th Infantry Brigade in GOUZEAUCOURT SECTOR (GONNELIEU SALIENT) **Disposition.** 2 Sections forward in GOUZEAUCOURT engaged on line work. 2 " at Head Quarter W.9.d.8.7. engaged on work in back area. Attached Works Company 2 Platoons GOUZEAUCOURT 2 Platoons at Head Quarter. **Work** General Trench work in Line: Revetting firebays, drainage & maintenance of Trenches. Construction of shelter for garrison in line and accommodation in rear. Construction of Trench Mortar emplacements, Gun and Stores HdQuarters etc. Work in back area. Erection of Hutted Camps, repair of roads, points and huts et.	O.B.R.
	2nd		General Trench work in line. Preparation of regimes for Raid on Corner Redoubt. leads to Trench Mines repaired. One Pad deliberately cut supposed enemy action.	O.B.R.
	3		General Field Work. 1 Lieut J.P. Leslie R.E. & 2 O.R. rejoin from hospital	O.B.R.
	4		General Trench work as m/1st. Capt. Saffers sent to Bycle Bonton School to practice raid. Officer of 10th Welsh Co. take over work preparation for Relief. 1 O.R. to hospital.	O.B.R.
	5		General Trench work. ordinary day. No wire obtain. Capt. Saffers gave Lecture Party 4/18 Welsh Regt. for raid on CORNER REDOUBT, taking Capt. Mobile Charges. 2 Bungalore Torpedoes. Party entered French Mt at 9.45 P.M. but only one cut holes to formed. This was blown in. Party returned safely 3 O.R. wounded, all duty. heads to Mines again cut Mines not exploded.	O.B.R.
	6.		General Trench work in line during day, with exercise in evening preparation to relief on 7th Inst. by 20th Division	O.B.R.

WAR DIARY
or
INTELLIGENCE SUMMARY.

(Erase heading not required.)

Army Form C. 2118.

OCTOBER 1917.   229th Field Coy RE

Place	Date	Hour	Summary of Events and Information	Remarks and references to Appendices
SORREL-LE-GRAND	Oct. 7.		Company relieved in the GOUZEAUCOURT SECTOR by C/6th Field C.E. R.E. 120th I.F. Bde. Works Coy. attached marched out of H.Q. in SUNKEN ROAD at 2.0 p.m. and moved into billets in SORREL-LE-GRAND. Outhouses & farms for billeting. Rest area. Proceeded by rail to PERONNE to go forward to GOUY-EN-ARTOIS with 120th I.F. Bde on 8th inst.	OBR
DOINGT	Oct. 8.		Effective Strength 2 offs. 203 O.R. including 6 O.R. detached & 2 O.R. on leave. Attached Infantry 2 offs. 13 O.R. 40 D.S.R.E. M.O. & 25 O.R. detached from Company. Transport and mounted personnel cyclists proceed by road to DOINGT. 3 inf 1 Adrian Ans & proceed by motor lorries to DOINGT. 1 O.R. with C.E. billeted with Coy's & attached Officers (Billet Sgt.) LT. England. 1 O.R. proceed to England as Officer (Billet Sgt.)	OBR
"	9.		Company resting - DOINGT. Capt. F.W. CLARK regains company for III Army Rest Camp. 2 O.R. rejoin fm III Army Rest Camp. 1 O.R. attached fm 231st Field Coy. R.E. and takes Command.	OBR
DOINGT	10		Coy. H.Q. & dismounted personnel + attached Works Coy. remain in DOINGT rest'n. Transport and mounted personnel join 119 I.F. Bde transport convoy at LE QUINCONCE at 7.30 A.M. and proceed by road to BAPAUME. Billeted in tents. 1 off 5 O.R with 1 waggon proceed by train fm PERONNE to BEAUMETZ-RIVIERE and join advance party at GOUY-EN-ARTOIS. 1 O.R. fm leave.	OBR
"	"		H.Q. & dismounted personnel with 120th I.F. Bde Works Coy proceed by road to PERONNE. Detrain at 8.30 A.M. at BEAUMETZ-RIVIERE proceed by road to GOUY-EN-ARTOIS. Billeted. Mule Lts. Transport mounted personnel leave BAPAUME at 7.30 A.M. and march to GOUY-EN-ARTOIS arriving at 2.30 p.m.	OBR

Army Form C. 2118.

WAR DIARY
or
INTELLIGENCE SUMMARY.
(Erase heading not required.)

OCTOBER 1917   229 Field Coy R.E.

Place	Date	Hour	Summary of Events and Information	Remarks and references to Appendices
Gouy-En-Artois	Oct. 12		Company constructed works - Company resting - Gouy.	O.B.R.
"	13		Work started on Camp in Divisional Area. Chiefly repair of Baths, Huts etc. 1 O.R. attached 40 Div. A.S.C. (Repairable) Effective Strength 3 off. 209 O.R. less 5. 7 O.R. detailed + 1 on leave. Attached Works 2 off. 159 O.R.	O.B.R.
"	14		Company attached Works O.R. in training sports - Drill. Physical training - Division area carried on. Work on Camp utilized as an "L4".	O.B.R.
"	15		2 O.R. to hospital 1 O.R. to hospital	
"	16		— do — Assistance in training	
"	17		Work & Training of 119 & 121 by O.R. Works companies was demanded & against & training. 1 offr. sent to 14 & — 1 offr. to 14 & 14 & S.B. Wiltshire. In these companies. lectures given: Rapid wiring, trench work etc.	O.B.R.
"	18		— do — 1 off. attached for return to 15th W. Yorkshire Regt.	O.B.R.
"	19		— do —	O.B.R.
"	20		— do — 1 off. — 7 O.R. detached 1 O.R. leave.	O.B.R.
			Effective Strength 8 off. 205 O.R. including 1 off. — 7 O.R. detached 1 O.R. leave. Attached Works 2 off. 155 O.R.	

Army Form C. 2118.

WAR DIARY
or
INTELLIGENCE SUMMARY.

(Erase heading not required.)

OCTOBER 1917. 225 Field Cy R.E.

Place	Date	Hour	Summary of Events and Information	Remarks and references to Appendices
GOUY-EN-ARTOIS.	Oct. 21		Lieut Cox attached works Coy in training at G.O.O.7. Drill, Gas drill ? Preparing Firing section on R.E. work etc. Work on repair of Butts & huts in Divisional Area. Repair of Rifle Range.	OBR
"	22		1 Off. & 10 O.R. proceed to England on leave. 1 O.R. to hospital.	OBR AR
"	23		Training Work a. a. 21" 4 Off. proceed to III Army Rest Camp.	OBR
"	24		do 1 Off. & regm fm 13th Y.&L. (ft duty with 121 Bde works Cy.)	AR
"	25		do 1 Off. transferred to Rifle Bde fm 23rd English Regt.	
"	26		do Preparatory order received for Coy. to move to POPERINGHE with 119th Fld Bde Group.	AR
"	27		Orders received for Advance party to proceed at 7.30h. with 119th Bde Advce party to billets in POPERINGHE. Order cancelled at 4.0h. Order re-issued at 5.0h. to start by to proceed at 7.30h order again cancelled. Orders received for transport & pipelines to proceed on 28" inst. to MOISLAINS. Thence on 29' to MOISLAINS.	OBR

Effective Strength 8 Off. 204 OR. Indlg: 9 OR. detached; 1 Off. 1 OR. on leave.

WAR DIARY
or
INTELLIGENCE SUMMARY

Army Form C. 2118.

229 Field Coy RE   October 1917

MAP 62c 1/40,000

Place	Date	Hour	Summary of Events and Information	Remarks and references to Appendices
GOUY-EN-ARTOIS.	Oct 28.		Transport & mounted personel with cyclists proceed by road to BAPAUME. Dismounted Personel prepare to leave for MOISLAINS on 29th inst.	CRE.
"	29.		Transport & mounted personel with cyclists leave BAPAUME at 7.30 am & proceed by road to MOISLAINS. Billets secured for Company in WARDEN CAMP nr. HAUT ALLAINES. Dismounted Personel Entrain at GOUY-EN-ARTOIS at 6.30 P.M. and proceed to PERONNE.	CRE.
WARDEN CAMP HAUT-ALLAINES (L.29.b.7.7.)	30		Dismounted Personel detrain at PERONNE at 12.15 A.M. and march to billets at WARDEN CAMP. Work on construction of Battalion Camp in MOISLAINS Valley under C.R.E. III Corps Troops.	CRE.
"	31		Work on Battalion Camp at MOISLAINS started. Preparation of sites, salvage of timber required for Accn. Huts, Transportation etc.	CRE.

O.B.Raynor Capt RE
OC 229 AUS TCRE

FOR 229 AUS TCRE

WAR DIARY
or
INTELLIGENCE SUMMARY

(Erase heading not required.)

Army Form C. 2118

229th FIELD Co RE.

NOVEMBER 1917

Place	Date	Hour	Summary of Events and Information	Remarks and references to Appendices
HAUT ALLAINES	Nov 1st		Coy attached to III Corps, working as Corps Troops under CRE Corps Troops. Billeted in WARDEN CAMP HAUT ALLAINES. Companies employed in erection of Brigade Camp at MOISLAINS - ADRIAN HUTS NISSEN HUTS and Camp accessories. Tramtrolline? pushing nettine from MURLU ROAD Cook Gums Latrines etc.	OBR
	2		Work as on 1st beds & Camp	OBR
	3		Work as on 1st	OBR
	4		Work as on 1st	OBR
	5		Work as on 1st	OBR
	6		Work as on 1st. 1 officer & 12 men proceed on leave.	OBR
	7		Work as on 1st	OBR
	8		Work as on 1st	OBR
	9		Work as on 1st	OBR
	10		Work as on 1st. Small scarlet coloured German gas balloon with Electric light attached fell in Co Lines. Handed in to III Corps Head Quarters.	OBR
	11		Work as on 1st	OBR
	12		One section visiting. Three Sections proceed to ETRICOURT to erect Battalion Camp between ETRICOURT and MANANCOURT.	OBR
	13		One Section erecting VARENNE ADRIAN huts in Brigade Camp at MOISLAINS. Remaining three Sections erecting III Army Huts at MANANCOURT. 6 officers on leave.	OBR
	14		Work as on 13th	OBR

WAR DIARY
or
INTELLIGENCE SUMMARY
(Erase heading not required.)

Army Form C. 2118

229th FIELD Coy. R.E.

NOVEMBER 1917

Place	Date	Hour	Summary of Events and Information	Remarks and references to Appendices
			MAP. FRANCE. 57c 1/40,000	
HAUT-ALLAINS	Nov.15		Work as on 13.	att2
	16		Work as on 13.	att2
	17		Work as on 13	att2
	18		Work as on 13. Orders received from III Corps to rejoin 119 Bde Group at BARASTRE. Coy to prepare to move.	att2
	19		HAUT-ALLAINS at 4.30 p.m. 19th Inst. 2 platoons 119 enfantry are to return to the Rum Estaircourt. Advance parties sent to BARASTRE.	att2
BARASTRE			Nos 1,2 & 3 Sections return to the Rum Estaircourt. Coy marches out of HAUT ALLAINES at 4.30 p.m. and proceeds by march route to BARASTRE. Billeted in Nissen Huts. 5. O.R. proceed on leave. 10 rejoin from III Corps H.Q.	att2
	20		One Section ordered to stand by to proceed with 119th Inf. Bde. in Advance Guard of IV Corps moving forward after main attack on HINDENBURG LINE. All blankets, great coats + surplus kit dumped. Rations for rapid movement. Obtained. 1 days iron ration issued. 1 air day forage for horses. Coy ordered to stand by to move forward at one hours notice. Coy stands by from 12 noon until midnight. 1 O.R. from Base.	att2
	21.		At 10.0 a.m. Coy ordered to move immediately to BEAUMETZ at BEAUMETZ by 3.0 p.m. and is ordered to report to 119 Yble. Coy sets off but is ordered to return to BEAUMETZ. Proceed to Doignies by pm 119 Bn. All. 1 O.R. to Hospital. 1 O.R. attached to 40 Div T.M. Bn. Billeted in BEAUMETZ.	att
BEAUMETZ LEZ-CAMBRAI J.20.a.2.7.	22		Coy employed in making a foot track across No Mans Land - the English line "no mans land" + old German line + W. CANAL. Track marked by pickets + tape.	att

Army Form C. 2118

WAR DIARY
or
INTELLIGENCE SUMMARY

(Erase heading not required.)

November 1914.   229 Houlstre   (3)

Map. Sheet 57c /40,000 FRANCE

Place	Date	Hour	Summary of Events and Information	Remarks and references to Appendices
BEAUMETZ LEZ-CAMBRAI V.10.a.2.7	22		Orders received at 4.0 p.m. that Coy is to proceed at 2.0 A.m. on 23rd Inst. to HAVRINCOURT. CO returns to billets at 7.30 p.m. to prepare to move out. 1 O.R. (Buntfield) accidentally injured 2 O.R. accidentally wounded by explosion of German bomb.	ORR
HAVRINCOURT K.27.b.6.3.	23		Coy marched out of BEAUMETZ and proceed to HAVRINCOURT & makes arrangements in Hindenburg Tunnel Owing to the very bad state of the road across the old No man's land between TRESCAULT and HAVRINCOURT the transport was c/r at Q.3.d.9.9. & failed to field. 1 off. returned from leave.	ORR
	24		After the attack by the 119 & 121 Inf Bdes of the 40th Division on BOURLON WOOD and BOURLON VILLAGE, Company moved towards the consolidate the position in the wood. G.O.C. 119th Inf Bde ordered the Company to consolidate in ANNEUX at 9.0 Am ready to consolidate when he gave the order. Orders given at 11.30 p.m. to consolidate position in centre of wood. Strong point eg 9 ent at E.13.b.3.9. and trench dug to 3'x3'. Work was much delayed by hostile fire. approachs were heavily shelled. 6 O.R. wounded during operations. 12 O.R. return from leave. Lieut. E.F. BOREL R.E. attached to 119th Inf Bde. Effective Strength 8 Off. 205 O.R. + 13 O.R. R.E. Liaison Officers	ORR
	25		Co again consolidating position = BOURLON WOOD. Strong points were layed out during hours of daylight = partially completed utilising old German trenches existing here and wiring the trees in front from strong points west of E.13.d. (2) F.2.7.d.2.2. (3) E.19.a.3.2. (4) E.14.c.3.3.	

1875   Wt. W.593/826   1,000,000   4/15   J.B.C. & A.   A.D.S.S./Forms/C.2118.

Army Form C. 2118

WAR DIARY
or
INTELLIGENCE SUMMARY

(Erase heading not required.) 229th Field Cy RE. 40° Div.

NOVEMBER 1917.

Instructions regarding War Diaries and Intelligence Summaries are contained in F.S. Regs., Part II. and the Staff Manual respectively. Title Pages will be prepared in manuscript.

Place	Date	Hour	Summary of Events and Information	Remarks and references to Appendices
HAVRINCOURT K.27.b.6.3.	Nov 26.		MAP FRANCE 57c 1/40,000. In view of the difficulty experienced in extending to forward trenches, the impossibility of capturing and holding BOURLON village decided to construct a main defensive line through BOURLON WOOD. Summary of strong points dug on 25.5. Tunnelled to avenue and started at F 7 d 22, one of the strong points engaged on trench-fighting before, extended it on the flanks, digging 150 yds of fire trench & wiring in front. Wire spikes transported to ANNEUX-CHAPEL dump (Bruce Stores). 1 OR killed 1 OR wounded.	CWR
	27		Strong point constructed at F.7.d.2.5. 2 OR killed 2 OR wounded	CWR
	28.		Strong point at F.7.d.1.5. wired. 1 OR wounded.	CWR
	29.		CO resting. Wire spikes carted to forward dump.	CWR
	30		CO employed on trench area work - repairing road from HAVRINCOURT to FLESQUIERES. Enemy counter attacks during morning at BOURLON WOOD & at GOUZEAUCOURT. All transport ordered to entrain south of HAVRINCOURT. Work kept up on roads. Billets - Nissen huts shelled during night. Orders rec'd during afternoon to stand by ready to move. CO stands by all night. C.R.Lawrence Capt. R.E. i/c 229 F.Cy RE	CWR

WAR DIARY

269th FIELD COMPANY, ROYAL ENGINEERS

DECEMBER 1917

VOL 19

SECRET

WAR DIARY
or
INTELLIGENCE SUMMARY

(Erase heading not required.)

Army Form C. 2118

229th FIELD Co. R.E.

DECEMBER 1917

Place	Date	Hour	Summary of Events and Information	Remarks and references to Appendices
HAVRINCOURT K.27.b.5.0.	Dec. 1.		Map 57c 1/40,000. FRANCE. Co. Billeted in Sugar Factory, HAVRINCOURT. Detached from Durham and employed on repair and maintenance of Roads — HAVRINCOURT - FLESQUIERES under C.R.E. 40th Div. Co. under orders to move at 16 notice to rejoin 16th Div. Effective Strength 8 off — 196 O.R. 8 O.R. rejoin from leave.	G.S.R.
"	2		Work on HAVRINCOURT - FLESQUIERES Rd as on 1st. Attached 1 off 30 O.R. to Hospital 2 O.R. to Hospital 1 off 19 O.R.	G.S.R.
"	3		Co R.E. 16th Div. in BULLECOURT SECTOR - gave instructions. Major F.W. CLARKE R.E. proceed to BEHAGNIES to take over work from 56 Field Co R.E. Orders received for Co to proceed to ST. LEGER on 4th. 8 O.R. rejoin from leave.	G.S.R.
ST. LEGER.	4		Dismounted personnel proceed by road via route to RUYAULCOURT and thence by motor bus to ST. LEGER. Transport and mounted personnel proceed by road to BERTINCOURT, BERVILLECOURT.	G.S.R.
"	5		Transport proceed to ST. LEGER. Work in Cme take over 2 free Sections & proceed to forward billets in CHALK PIT T 19 a. O.B. Major CLARKE R.E. proceeds to BLENDECQUES to GHQ RE School. A.C.R. region for leave. Co. in charge BULLECOURT SECTOR wide 119 Inf Bde.	G.S.R.
"	6		2/Lt. DURSTON attached to C.R.E. General trench work = Keeping ammunition Division Huts Hdg officer belvoir Support front line opening of frontline wheeled boards. Improvement of posts. Wiring of Support & Intermediate Line. Siting & construction of Intermediate line. One Section in reserve employed on construction & repair of water points, dug-outs etc in the Drummond area. 7 O.R. attached to Carpenters for work. 1 O.R. to Hospital. 1 O.R. Rejoined. 119 dubbs Work Coys.	G.S.R.
"	7		Work in Cmd as on 6th. hr.	Attached 1 off 195 O.R.
"	8		Work as on 6th hr.	Attached 1 off 77 O.R.

(Initials) Effective Strength 8 off 195 O.R.
Detached 2 off 13 O.R. Leave 4 O.R.

WAR DIARY
or
INTELLIGENCE SUMMARY

Army Form C. 2118

(Erase heading not required.) 229th Field Co. R.E.

DECEMBER 1917

MAP FRANCE. Sheet 57c 1/40,000. 51 1/40,000

Place	Date	Hour	Summary of Events and Information	Remarks and references to Appendices
ST. LEGER B42.6.8	Dec 9		Work as on 6th inst. Men of F Corps R.E. proceeded to camp of Infantry 1 O.R. to hospital. Forwarded billets to each gas shelled during night of 7/8. No casualties.	A.2
	10		Work as on 6th inst. Found billet agon. Receiving & sheltered during night. 1 O.R. to hospital.	A.2
	11		Work in Line as on 6th inst. 1 O.R. granted leave. 1 O.R. to hospital.	A.2
	12		Work = Line as on 6th inst. Work on trench tramways to forward areas. Maintenance and repairs.	A.2
	13		Work as on 6th inst. Construction of Run-Bot-Stores for Battalion in line commenced. Puts of 1 W.O. + 25 O.R. selected to assist Infantry in Raid on NEPTUNE TRENCH U21a. Meeting with Inf. Officers. 1 O.R. to hospital. Preparation made for R.E. cooperation in Infantry raid on R.E. to follow Raiding Party works up for conf. as if crossing trench, like Raiding parties meets & blow up after securing trench & clearing dug-outs in centre.	A.2
	14		Work as on 13th inst.	A.2
	15		Work in line as on 14th. Raid on Enemy trench (NEPTUNE TRENCH) = U21.a. 1 Off + 25 R.E. with charges accompanied infantry to two pushed Artillery + T.M. Barrage parties attacked along enemy trench and met in centre. 3 dug-outs found open, were seen in. The remainder had been previously destroyed by the enemy	A.2

Army Form C. 2118.

WAR DIARY
or
INTELLIGENCE SUMMARY.
(Erase heading not required.)

229th Field Coy R.E. (3)

DECEMBER 1917

Place	Date	Hour	Summary of Events and Information	Remarks and references to Appendices
ST. LEGER. B.A.a.6.8.	15.		Consolidation of Captured front and new posts of front line was proceeded with at dusk. Two strong points covering wire line wired. Effective Strength 8 officers 198 OR (include 3 off 16 OR detached 22 OR General attached 1 off 7 OR.	AP1
	16		General trench work. Consolidation & wiring of new strong points & new front line. 1 OR transferred to signals.	AP1
	17.		General trench work as on 16". A German Counter Strong point ("ARBOR") at U 20 d 9-7 in NO MAN'S LAND evacuated by enemy and to raid on 17-15 was blown up by a R.E. party at 6·0 A.M. Construction of a trench foot transport tram for Battalion in the line commenced. 7 OR on leave. 2 other Ranks East. Work done as before.	AP1
	18		Work as on 18. No 1070999 Cpl. F. BRUCE Returned is deputation.	AP1
	19.			AP2
	20.		Work as on 18. No 2 Sect. relieved in line by No 3. No 2 became Section in reserve. B OR proceed on leave. 1 OR on leave. 1 OR on business.	AP1
	21.		Instructions given that all available men of Infantry & RE should concentrate on wiring front support and intermediate line on 22 - 23 inst but repetition made for using further dumps of wiring material established.	AP2

Tree work as on 20 —

WAR DIARY or INTELLIGENCE SUMMARY

Army Form C. 2118.

229 FIELD Coy. 2

DEC. 1917

Place	Date	Hour	Summary of Events and Information	Remarks and references to Appendices
ST. LEGER B.9.a.6.9	Dec. 22		All front work and work in back areas cancelled. Except work in Cemetery & Coy H.Q. Trench foot room. Coy employed in wiring the Stop & Intermediate lines. A carrying party in connection with Brigade front. Effective strength — 8 off. 201 OR including 3 off. 12 OR detached, 2 off. 52 OR on leave. Allocated 1 — 80 OR	C.27
	23.		Wiring continued. Three up belts put out tonight before wiring by engineers of Coy H.Q. for kept Bruell's. One section taken off, 1 OR wounded in action.	C.31
	24.		Work as on 23. 1 OR on leave. 1 OR from hospital.	C.32
	25.		(As allowed) Break except no employed.	C.33
	26.		General trench work resumed. Work much hindered too cold for operation. Nos. 1 & 2 sections busy at front making [illegible] for gun positions. 2 Lt. P.E. EASTON RE returned — also remain at dub	C.34
	27		[crossed out] wounded	C.35 [C.36]
	29.		General trench work. Parties with charges sent out with infantry patrols to destroy abandoned German concrete pill boxes in no man's land. One Pill box was blown up with M.G. Emplacement with deep dug out destroyed.	C.36

Army Form C. 2118.

WAR DIARY
or
INTELLIGENCE SUMMARY.

(Erase heading not required.)

229 FIELD C⁰ R.E.   (5)

DEC 1917

Place	Date	Hour	Summary of Events and Information	Remarks and references to Appendices
ST LEGER	Dec 29		General trench work. Erection of new Camp for D.R.C. 7 O.R. on leave. 1 O.R. sent to VIII Army Hyp School for course of training.	ABR
	30		Took an "OP". Party of Sappers sent on not to Paris to destroy abandoned German MG Emplacement (cements) and deep dug-out - old German trench. MG cliffs + dug out blown up. MAJOR F W CLARKE RE assumes command of Company. N⁰ 105207 Sgt. CARTWRIGHT H & N⁰ 106813 L/CPL WALKER awarded the Military Medal for gallantry during raid on enemy trench on August 15ᵗʰ inst.	ABR ABR
	31		General Trench work as in "29". Work for Corps.	

O.B.Rayner
Capt R.E. A/O.C.
for O.C. 229

VA 20

229th FIELD Coy R.E.

War Diary – January 1918

Vol. 10

CONFIDENTIAL

Army Form C. 2118.

WAR DIARY
or
INTELLIGENCE SUMMARY.

(Erase heading not required.)

229th FIELD Cy R.E.

JANUARY 1918.

Instructions regarding War Diaries and Intelligence Summaries are contained in F.S. Regs., Part II. and the Staff Manual respectively. Title pages will be prepared in manuscript.

Place	Date	Hour	Summary of Events and Information	Remarks and references to Appendices
ST. LEGER.	JAN 1st		Company working in line with 119th Infantry Brigade in BULLECOURT SECTOR. Disposition: 3 Sections in Line work in forward billets near CROISELLES HQ, O.R.s and one section on Back Area work in ST. LEGER. Situation in line normally quiet with occasional moderate enemy shelling in places. Work in Line: Improvement of front line trench and posts — opening up, clearing + trench boarding recelled. Communication between supp.t line and front line being cleared. Acceptance given to Infants of trivilising excavation chiefly + dgt. Pub seats. Work in 1st dam. It was possible to use the Tunnel in Tunnel Trench for excavation. Reserve & Comm. Gen Sites. Trench for treatm.t of Rams. Maintenance of Trench tramlines etc. Wiring of Support areas. Work: Gun Emm.s construct.d by H/Section + stable of M.Gun + New Bethy + Trench for treatm.t room. Work: Back Areas. General repairs. Shutting + banks + provision of beds + treatm.t	O.R.
	" 2.		Guards: MAJOR F.W. CLARK R.E. & LIEUT E.F. BORRETT R.E. awarded the M.C. Work in line as on 1st.	O.R.
	" 3.		Work in line as on 1st.	O.R.
	" 4.		Work in line as on 1st. Working parties in front line interfered with by enemy shelling. CROISELLES shelled with H.E. & R.G. Work on GOUZEAUCOURT much interrupted by hostile shelling. Trench mat. changed — hvy G.	O.R.S
	" 5.		Work: sitn. as on 1st.	O.R.S
	6		Visit by Straight units. 8th 199 O.R. including 2 off 9 O.R. detailed & 1 off 39 O.R. on leave. Attached Infants. 1 off 75 O.R. Work in Line as on 1st. Work commenced on ARRAS-BAPAUME Rd. Ammunition dump to project W. against Aerial bombs. Wall yard round dump thrown up.	

2353 Wt. W2544/1454 700,000 5/15 D.D. & L. A.D.S.S./Fortns/C. 2118.

WAR DIARY or INTELLIGENCE SUMMARY

Army Form C. 2118.

229th Field Coy R.E.

January 1918

Place	Date	Hour	Summary of Events and Information	Remarks and references to Appendices
			MAP. FRANCE Sheet 57c/1/40,000	
ST LEGER	Jan 7		Work in Coy area 1st Bn obtained on Co's Billets. St Leger shelled by H.V. gun at about 7.30 p.m. Two direct hits on Co's Billets 5 O.R. wounded. Frost still holding though not very severe. Work is possible in the trenches particularly when deep but is difficult on the surface. Occasional temporary thaws during the preceding days have not caused any serious effect in the trenches. Efforts being made to get all trenches cleared & revetted where possible (particularly communication trenches) before the thaw sets in. Main forward communication is Eff. Previous unrevetted Revetting started with A frames & concrete Sandbags. Shellfire put up 40 ft of very line.	ARR
"	" 8		Work as on 7th	ARR
"	" 9		Work as on 7th	
"	" 10		Work as on 7th. Information received to effect that enemy may shortly carry out an attack in the Bullecourt sector. Preparation for R.E. action as usual & working parties in case of enemy under orders of Div. Commander. R.E. in trenches to withdraw line.	ARR
"	" 11		Work in Coy as usual. Ambulance given to T.M.A. in sector of Gorblecks.	ARR
"	" 12		Work in Coy as usual. Effective strength of Coy 8 off 197 O.R. including 2 off 105 details ARR. 2 off 41 O.R. on leave. Attached party (Works Company) 1 off 75 O.R.	ARR
"	" 13		Work in Coy as usual. Thaw setting in causing crumbling obliteration of each of trench walls. Loose material	CAR

Army Form C. 2118.

WAR DIARY
or
INTELLIGENCE SUMMARY.

(Erase heading not required.) 229th FIELD COY R.E.

MAP. FRANCE Sheet 57C 1/40,000. JANUARY 1918.

Place	Date	Hour	Summary of Events and Information	Remarks and references to Appendices
ST. LEGER T.25.a.7.1.	JAN 13th		Falling into trenches. Work in Cmy. became usual.	Q131 £131
	" 14		Work in Cmy as usual. Condition of trenches particularly Communication Trench is very bad. A large amount of work must be spent if men are to move by trench in many places, as foulus in the acting of the Coy front has in several feet deep - mud.	CXR
	16.		Condition of trenches very bad indeed where not revetted. The trenches have fallen in & are almost impassable. The labour of clearing has become altogether beyond the powers of the permanent trench parties. It is decided to employ every available man — R.E. Pioneers & Infantry in clearing the Communication & working parties from the Bn's, leaving the trenches at night & throwing up the mud etc. from bottom of trenches by day. Front line trenches to be left to garrison to clear. Tracks made - marked by tape - across the top to afford access to C.n.5.	NBR
			China trenches were revetted with A frames and corrugated iron & wire. Expanded metal held in by timber runners between A frames. The sides stood up perfectly steep in a few places but were pressed in, A frames, due to very wet soil by burst Mol CI & higher explosive. Place to A frames.	

WAR DIARY
or
INTELLIGENCE SUMMARY.

Army Form C. 2118.

(Erase heading not required.)

22nd NEW CORPS

JANUARY 1918.

Place	Date	Hour	Summary of Events and Information	Remarks and references to Appendices
St. LÉGER	Jan 16	Mpt MANOR Pt. 57c /A0000	were only backed by Expanded metal unsupported by runners at the present of the wet earth. In many cases Exp: metal clue heads were weak, well bermed & revetted at bottom with ample men and Expanded metal the have stood very well. Narrow unrevetted trenches collapsed where unparapeted. BATTLE ZONE One section took off from line work to site, lay out wiring & dig a pinted trench ECOUST SWITCH forming the first out Second Line of the Battle Zone. Forms a defensive flank in case to village of ECOUST was captured. Trench to be Coy S at as a fire trench. Fire bays 30' long. Traverses 15' x 12'. Wiring to be single apron fence.	A.S.R.
"	17		Work concentrated on clearing of main lines of communication	C.S.R.
"	18		Work as on 17. Site for duckboard track across the top chosen on right flank to take the place of the main communication trench on right. These boards carried up to forward dumps in readiness.	A.S.R.
"	19		Work as on 17. Duckboard track on right laid. 700 yds long. Buoy's new built.	A.S.R.

Army Form C. 2118.

WAR DIARY
or
INTELLIGENCE SUMMARY.

(Erase heading not required.) 22cd Bull C.R.E.

JAN. 1918.

Instructions regarding War Diaries and Intelligence Summaries are contained in F. S. Regs., Part II. and the Staff Manual respectively. Title pages will be prepared in manuscript.

Place	Date	Hour	Summary of Events and Information	Remarks and references to Appendices
St LEGER	Jan 19.		Effective Strength of Unit: Officers 8, Infantry Other Ranks 197, OR detached 14, OR leave 14, OR sick, 11, OR Company 2, 1 OR 76 OR.	AA1.
	20		Work in line as in 19. Through communication established on left to support line. Main communication from support to front line was never completed throughout with A frames. Dual board tunnel continued Adv s/s of head chg to 18" deep in ECOUST switch. Infantry fighting pump work as in 19.	AB1.
	21		Work as in 19.	AB2.
	22		Work as in 19. Approval to new entrance of tunnel cleared opening access to tunnel now used for accommodation.	AB2.
	23			AB2.
	24		Work as in line as usual. Two main communications open on left. Tunnel communication to front line on extreme left started - would be cleared.	AB2.
	25		Work - line as usual.	
	26		Dual board track on left Capel between support line and front line (jumping) alternative communication between the two tunnels.	AB2.
	27.		Work - line as usual. Main communication on right shell closed & we decided to excavate work on this tunnel for three days to open	AB2.

2353 Wt. W3511/1454 700,000 5/15 D. D. & L. A.D.S.S./Form/C. 2118.

Army Form C. 2118.

WAR DIARY
or
INTELLIGENCE SUMMARY.

(Erase heading not required.) 224 FdCoyRE

JAN. 1918.

Place	Date	Hour	Summary of Events and Information	Remarks and references to Appendices
St LEGER	26		Effective Strength B off 202 OR. Wks & details 1 off 9 or + 2 off 36 OR on leave	WDR
			Attached wJAth Trench Wks Cn - 1 off 73 OR.	
	27		Work on Henry T.M. Emplacements started Construction of Cl HQ + Cine resumed.	
			Work in line am 26" ECOUST Gen.R. shelled. R.E. dump set a fire & destruction	WDR
			site for new communication trench between Front & Support lines a slight cleaver.	
	28		Work on new Communication trench in night	
			to front line.	
			Enemy aircraft bombed St LEGER at about 7.20 h. No damage caused.	WDR
	29		Work as usual. New Forward Communication trench end and + tapes.	
	30		Work in line Concentrated on new Communication trench in repair.	
	31		Work as on 30"	

OxPryor RE
CaptnRE
OC 224 FdCoyRE

WAR DIARY.

229th Field Company R.E.

FEBRUARY 1918   Vol. 21

CONFIDENTIAL

Army Form C. 2118.

WAR DIARY
or
INTELLIGENCE SUMMARY
(Erase heading not required.)

229th FIELD COY R.E. 40th Div.

FEBRUARY 1918

MAP. FRANCE Sheet 57c /40000.

Place	Date	Hour	Summary of Events and Information	Remarks and references to Appendices
St. Leger B.4.a.9.7.	Feb.1.		Company working in the Bullecourt Sector with the 119th Inf. Bde. – the Right Bde. of the 40th Div. Company Headquarters, transport and one Reserve Section in St. Leger. Three Sections employed or have been billeted in the Chalk Pit near Croisilles. Company engaged on general trench work in the line and billet repairs & improvements in the Divisional back area, also on construction of defence work in New Battle Zone. Trench work: The trenches generally in fair condition following the recent keen weather. The main communication trenches had been cleaned and communication established to the front line. The front line and Support line were being gradually cleaned and already been made good. Provision of new accommodation in the form of T.M. Emplacements and protection against gas were been carried out. All R.E. work is being continued on New Battle Zone. One Section engaged in laying out and wiring Ecoust Switch. Work in back area. The majority of the R.E. work (excluding skilled labour) over on Feb. 1st is to the field Companies of the Division which is about (relative to 40th) work etc. as on 1st.	Apl.
	Feb. 2.		Effective Strength of Company (weekly statement) 8 off. 203 O.R. including 1 off. 8 OR. detached and 2 off. 37 O.R. on leave. Attached Works Cos. (Infantry) 1 off. 7 OR. OR.	
	" 3		Work etc. as on 1st.	

Army Form C. 2118.

WAR DIARY
or
INTELLIGENCE SUMMARY.

(Erase heading not required.)

229th FIELD COY. R.E.

FEBRUARY 1918.

Place	Date	Hour	Summary of Events and Information	Remarks and references to Appendices
ST. LEGER. B.4.a.9.7.	Feb. 4		Map. FRANCE. Sheet 57c/40000. Work in line, on Battle Zone and on Back Area as on 1st.	CRE
"	5		Work in line etc. as on 1st.	CRE
"	6		Work in line etc. as on 1st. One H. & 7 OR. of 470 Field Coy R.E. attached to C.P. to receive families with no Section.	CRE
"	7		Work in line as on 1st.	CRE
"	8		Work " line " " "	CRE
"	9		Work " line " " 1st. Effective Strength (weekly state) 8 off. 205 OR. include 1 off. 13 OR. detached, 2 & 31 OR. on leave. 11C of bde. works CF (attached) (Infantry) 1 off. 48 OR.	CRE
"	10		Work in line as on 1st. Drainage and improvement of water points in St. LEGER. Reserved of 11C H by Bde. works Coy rejoin their Brigades.	CRE
"	11		Work in left Bde Area BULLECOURT Sector handed over to 470th Field Coy 59th Div.n 3 P.M. Sappers returned from forward billets to ST. LEGER. 3 O.R. rejoined from leave. 2 O.R. to hospital sick.	FWE
HENIN N32a.3.4.	12		Coy H.Q. and four sections proceeded to HENIN - transport, less tool cart, limbers and water cart to MORY (B28a.4.6). Coy HQ HENIN N32a.3.4. 4 O.R. leave to UK. 20 O.R. rejoined from leave, 1 O.R. from 40th Divl. Sigs, 10 O.R. from H.Q. R.E. 40th Div.n	FWE

Army Form C. 2118.

WAR DIARY
or
INTELLIGENCE SUMMARY.
(Erase heading not required.)

Instructions regarding War Diaries and Intelligence Summaries are contained in F. S. Regs., Part II. and the Staff Manual respectively. Title pages will be prepared in manuscript.

Place	Date	Hour	Summary of Events and Information	Remarks and references to Appendices
HENIN N32a.3.4.	Feb. 13.		O.'s of Coy cleaning up kit and equipment. Officers and senior N.C.O.'s reconnoitring lines for new work on left sector VI Corps Battle Area.	flu.
	14		Morning, drill, gas protective appliance inspection. Afternoon games. 2 O.R. to hospital (sick) - 7 O.R. rejoined from leave, 1 O.R. joined Coy from leave	flu.
	15.		Morning drill & kit cart inspection. Afternoon, games. 4 O.R. leave to U.K., 1 O.R. attached N°8 R.E. Park with pontoons 7 Coy Bridging gear. 1 O.R. returned from hospital	flu.
	16		Morning drill & kit cart inspection. Afternoon games. 1 O.R. to hospital (sick), 6 O.R. rejoined from leave. Effective strength 8 Officers 206 O.R. Detached, 1 officer and 14 O.R. - on leave 1 Officer, 26 O.R.	flu.
	17		Morning, drill. Work commenced 6-0 p.m. on firing line third system VI Corps Battle Line. 600 Infantry working party. 1 O.R. attached Heavy Bridging School AIRE - 1 O.R. from hospital.	flu.

2353 Wt. W2544/1454 700,000 5/15 D. D. & L. A.D.S.S./Forms/C. 2118.

WAR DIARY
or
INTELLIGENCE SUMMARY.

Army Form C. 2118.

Place	Date	Hour	Summary of Events and Information	Remarks and references to Appendices
HENIN N32a.3.4.	Feb. 18.		Morning, dull. Work resumed in evening 6-0 p.m. on fixing line third system VIth Corps Battle Zone. 600 Infantry Working Party. 3.O.R. granted leave to U.K. – 1.O.R. to hospital (sick)	Ylve.
	19.		Morning, dull. Work resumed in evening. Sappers out only – no I.W.P. available. Sappers employed in wiring line dug to 3' on 14th, 15th, 18th and trimming up trench. Lieut. J.P. LESLIE & 2.O.R. granted leave to U.K. – Capt. A.B. RAYNER and 3.O.R. rejoined from leave.	Ylve.
	20.		Morning, dull. Work resumed in evening in VIth Corps Battle Zone. Post C24 commanding WANCOURT VILLAGE & VALLEY opened out, VALLEY wired. 600 Infantry Working Party. 1.O.R. rejoined from leave, 1.O.R. to hospital (sick) – Capt. A.B. RAYNER proceeded to MORY horse lines relieving 2nd Lieut. BENNETT who rejoined Coy at HENIN.	Ylve.
	21.		C.R.E. 40th Divn inspected Coy at 11-30 a.m. Work continued 6-0 p.m. on C24 Post and deepening C.T. from post to MENINEL SWITCH commenced. 600 Infantry Working Party. I.O. rejoined from VI Corps Infantry School – 1.O.R. leave to U.K.	Ylve.

Army Form C. 2118.

WAR DIARY
or
INTELLIGENCE SUMMARY.
(Erase heading not required.)

Instructions regarding War Diaries and Intelligence Summaries are contained in F. S. Regs., Part II. and the Staff Manual respectively. Title pages will be prepared in manuscript.

Place	Date	Hour	Summary of Events and Information	Remarks and references to Appendices
HENIN N32.a.3.4.	Feb. 22		Half C'oy out daywork straightening up and setting out tasks etc. on VI-th Corps Battle Zone work. Work resumed 6.0 p.m. on HENINEL SWITCH C.T. from Post C24 to HENINEL SWITCH. Infantry Working Party of 600. 1 O.R. rejoined from hospital, 4 O.R. from leave, - 1 O.R. to hospital (sick).	ffwl
	23.		Half C'oy out daywork as on 22nd. Work resumed 6.0 pm on HENINEL SWITCH C.T. from Post C24 to HENINEL SWITCH, work commenced on HENINEL SWITCH. Infantry Working Party of 600. Effective strength 8 officers, 201 O.R. - detached officers and 1 O.R. - on leave 1 officer, ? 18 O.R. - 3 O.R. joined C'oy from leave.	ffwl
	24		Half C'oy out daywork as before. Work resumed 6.0 pm. on HENINEL SWITCH. Infantry Working Party of 600. 4 O.R. granted leave to U.K. 2nd Lieut. E.R. BENNETT and 2 O.R. att'd VI-th Corps Infantry School.	ffwl
	25		Half C'oy out daywork as before. Scheduled task - 1000 x frontage - of HENINEL SWITCH completed to 3' deep and 60% wired. Task conveyed to sites for fresh work. Infantry working party of 600. N.B. Average task on work from Feb.14th to 25th inclusive = 53 cubic feet per man digging. Much of this includes deepening partially dug lines. 4 O.R. rejoined from leave	ffwl

Army Form C. 2118.

WAR DIARY
or
INTELLIGENCE SUMMARY.

(Erase heading not required.)

Instructions regarding War Diaries and Intelligence Summaries are contained in F. S. Regs., Part II. and the Staff Manual respectively. Title pages will be prepared in manuscript.

Place	Date	Hour	Summary of Events and Information	Remarks and references to Appendices
HENIN N32a.3.4.	Feb. 26		Half Coy on Daywork as before. Special working party at 6.0 p.m. of 600 for digging reserve line 2nd system VIth Corps Battle Zone in addition to normal 600, giving a total of 1200 o.r. 1350' frontage of this line dug to 18" deep and beamed. Average excavation per man = 7.8 cubic feet. Trace of trench [diagram showing trench dimensions: 29', 15', 7', 15', 7', 7'] All spoil thrown on parapet and 3' berm cleared.	JWC
	27.		Sappers cleaning up tools, handing in same to BOYELLES DUMP.	JWC
	28		Coy moved from HENIN & MORY by road to BARLY (ARRAS). Left HENIN 7-20 a.m., four sections with their transport. Remainder of transport left MORY 7-30 a.m. and joined sections West of ADINFER. Arrived BARLY 3-20 p.m. No one fell out.	JWC

Hollah Major R.E.
O.C. 229 Feb. Field Coy R.E.
28/2/18

40th Divisional Engineers

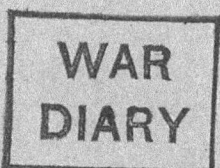

229th FIELD COMPANY R.E.

MARCH 1 9 1 8

WAR DIARY or INTELLIGENCE SUMMARY

Army Form C. 2118.

229th FIELD Coy. R.E. 40th Div.

MARCH 1918.

Place	Date	Hour	Summary of Events and Information	Remarks and references to Appendices
BARLEY	Mar.1		Coy billetted in BARLY resting after march on February 28th.	O.R.R.
	2		Coy resting. Inspection parades for equipment clothing etc. Orders received to proceed on 3.3.18 to HENDICOURT with 119" Inf. Bde Group to be nearer to line in case of enemy attack on VI Corps or neighbouring Corps front. Div. still in G.H.Q. reserve.	O.R.R.
HENDICOURT	3		Coy paraded at 10.0 A.M. and marched to HENDICOURT.	O.R.R.
	4		Coy resting. Training programme arranged — Drill lecture Rifle practice etc.	O.R.R.
	5		Coy Training. Squad & rifle drill. Box Respirator drill. Lectures and instruction in use of Technical Instruments. (Compasses level etc)	O.R.R.
	6		Coy Training as on 5th. Instruction in Pontoon work.	O.R.R.
	7		Coy Training as on 5th & 6th. Particular attention paid to Gas drill.	O.R.R.
	8		Inspection by G.O.C. VI Corps. The G.O.C. addressed the troops congratulating them on the work previously done.	O.R.R.
	9		Coy Training as on 5th & 6th. Pontoons & Bridging Equipment dumped at HENDICOURT under guard. Firing Practice on Range. Instructions received to move forward to BOISLEUX ST MARC on 12.3.18 to be in immediate reserve in readiness for expected German attack.	O.R.R.
	10		"	O.R.R.
	11		move forward to BOISLEUX ST MARC.	O.R.R.
BOISLEUX-ST-MARC	12		Coy paraded & proceeded to BOISLEUX ST. MARC. with 119" Bde Gp. and is held in readiness to move off at 3 hours notice from 8.0 A.M. — 8.0 P.M. and ½ hrs. notice from 8.0 P.M. to 8.0 A.M.	O.R.R.
	13		Coy Training proceeded with in Camp.	O.R.R.
	14		"	O.R.R.
	15		Practice alarm at given at 6.50 A.M. Company ready to move off at 8.19 A.M.	O.R.R.
	16		Training Programme proceeded with.	O.R.R.

WAR DIARY
or
INTELLIGENCE SUMMARY.

229TH Fld. Coy. R.E. 40TH DIVISION.

MARCH 1918.

Place	Date	Hour	Summary of Events and Information	Remarks and references to Appendices
BOISLEUX-ST-MARC.	MAR.17		Training program proceeded with as in 15-16. Rifle ranges repaired. Owing to Coy. Butts ranges had become dangerous due to overs. Butts raised.	O.R.
"	18		Work continued on Rifle Range.	O.R.
"	19		" " " " "	O.R.
"	20		" " " " "	O.R.
"	21.	5.45 AM	German attack developed early in morning. Warning order received at 5.45 A.M. Company immediately stands to ready to move forward in support if attack succeeds.	
		1.28 PM	Orders received to move to HAMELINCOURT.	
		8.0 "	Coy marches out and arrives at ARMAGH CAMP HAMELIN COURT at 8.45 P.M. Orders received to man a section of the Army Line near ARRAS BAPAUME Rd. East of HAMELINCOURT at 4.0 A.M. on 22nd.	
		3.50 AM	Coy takes over section of Army Line in A.6.b. & A.1.a. ARRAS BAPAUME ROAD at 4.0 A.M. Post established. Patrols sent out. Road into ST LEGER and CROISELLES patrolled by Cyclist. Transport remains in HAMELINCOURT until 6.0 P.M. when it is ordered back to DOUCHY LES AYETTE.	O.R.
IN LINE near BEHAGNIES.	23rd	7.45 AM	Company relieved in Army Line by the GUARDS Bgde 31st Div. and moved back to man the old German Trench west of BEHAGNIES. - H.1.a. all day consolidate position. Coy stands to.	
		5.0 PM	Out 5.0 P.M. as situation was quiet. Coy moved down into tents in A.30.d.	
		9.45 PM	Coy moved out + dug 5 posts on Sewell System between GOMIECOURT ERVILLERS. Coy was relieved by 11-224 Field Coy R.E. and moved through BEHAGNIES and GOMIECOURT enroute through H.1. & T.C. ERVILLERS.	O.R.

for A.1.a. (22nd March) and read:
L.22.c.s B.1.a.

WAR DIARY
or
INTELLIGENCE SUMMARY.

(Erase heading not required.)

229th FIELD Coy. R.E. 40th DIVISION

MARCH 1918.

(3)

Place	Date	Hour	Summary of Events and Information	Remarks and references to Appendices
	23.		Transport moved back to BUCQUOY on BUCQUOY – MONCHY-LE-BOIS ROAD.	ABR.
	24.		Coy in tents between BEHAGNIES & GOMIECOURT resting. Took cart with technical equipment moved up to Coy billets in readiness for any Engineerwork. Forward transport shelled out of position in GOMIECOURT. Horses brought forward to billeats. Work recommenced on recent Septr line – A.30.d. & A.30.a. 1300 yds barbed wire fence erected.	ABR.
		11.0p.	Transport moved back to BUCQUOY. Company were rested (sunken) in A.22.b. in view of heavy hostile attack on ERVILLER'S Front.	
COURCELLES	25.	5.30a.m.	Coy were hurried again to position in A.30.d. & A.22.b. Coy ordered back to COURCELLES & withdrew to trench N.W. of COURCELLES held by A.27 Field Coy 41 Division. Coy shelled out of Camp in COURCELLES at 1.30p. held there until relieved at 3.30p.m. Coy marches to MONCHY-AU-BOIS arriving at 7.0 p.m. Transport withdrawn to MONCHY-AU-BOIS.	ABR.
MONCHY-AU-BOIS.	26.		Coy leave MONCHY-AU-BOIS at 7.30A.M. and marches to BIENVILLERS. It was reported by C.R.E. at noon that enemy had broken through at HEBUTERNE and was advancing to Armoured Cars from SOUTH. C.R.E. ordered Major CLARK R.E. to take Command of dispersed of BIENVILLERS and in conjunction with Infantry to organise defence of the village, and arrange for destruction of communication from the SOUTH.	ABR.

INTELLIGENCE SUMMARY.
229TH FIELD Coy. R.E. 40TH Division.
MARCH 1918.

Place	Date	Hour	Summary of Events and Information	Remarks and references to Appendices
BIENVILLERS.	26.		Ground was reconnoitred and Company immediately commenced to put the village into a state of defence. The old trenches South of village were improved, five strong houses barricaded and loopholed. M.G. emplacements constructed to fire on roads obstructions made by 231st Field C./R.E. Transport moved to POMMIER out 7.30 p.m. Situation was reported normal. C₂'s & transport were therefore withdrawn to original camp on N.W. of village. Orders received to proceed to GOUY EN ARTOIS on morning of 27 to be cleared BIENVILLERS by 8.0 A.M.	ASL.
	27.		Cy leaves BIENVILLERS at 2.0 A.M. and proceed by road route to GOUY-EN-ARTOIS arriving at 5.0 A.M. Cy move out of GOUY at 4.0 p.m. proceed to SOMBRIN arriving at 5.30 p.m. and is again inspected with M.G. by B.E. Group. During Evening Transport Lines bombed by German Aircraft.	ASL.
GOUY EN ARTOIS.	28.		Cy resting at SOMBRIN. Orders received to move 17th Army Area.	
SOMBRIN.	29		Cy leaves SOMBRIN at 8.26 A.M. + proceed to LaCOMTÉ by hand reentraining at 4.30 p.m.	CRM
	30		Cy Resting.	
	31.		Cy Resting. Orders received to move to IV Corps Area re-pBEITHUNE and unexpired part of a division in the line there. Detailed orders not received.	ASL

ARoyle Capt. R.E.
O.C. 229 Field C.R.E.

40th Divisional Engineers.

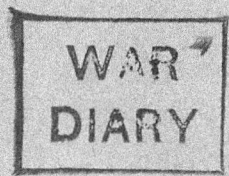

229th FIELD COMPANY R. E.

APRIL 1918

Vol 23

WAR DIARY.

229th FIELD COMPANY R.E.

Vol. 22.

APRIL 1918.

SECRET

Weekly State of Strength to be started again.
3.5.18.

Army Form C. 2118.

WAR DIARY
or
INTELLIGENCE SUMMARY.

(Erase heading not required.) 229ᵀ FIELD Coy R.E. 40ᵗʰ DIVISION.

APRIL 1918.

Place	Date	Hour	Summary of Events and Information	Remarks and references to Appendices
RUE PROVOST	Apr. 1		Company in staging area during march from III Army Area to take over front of ARMENTIERES sector — 1st Army Area. Dismounted personnel in RUE PROVOST near NEUF BERQUIN and Transport and mounted personnel at ECQUEDECQUES near LILLERS.	ARL
			Company moves forward into BAC ST MAUR G.18.b.8.6. and takes over quarters vacated by A.27 Field Coy R.E. Company in Divisional Engineer Reserve. ARMENTIERES Sector. O.C. A.27 Field Coy R.E. hands over work on paper.	
BAC ST MAUR G.18 b.8.6.	"2		Work in Reserve area commenced. Chief work — control of demolition stores for permanent bridges over the River Lys — maintenance of pontoon bridges and construction and camouflage of Cork Emergency Infantry Bridges (4) between BAC ST MAUR and SAILLY SUR-LA-LYS. Demolition parties told off and instructed in their duties, demolition stores checked and work started on Cork Emergency bridge. Construction of Artillery Emergency Tracks from BAC - ST MAUR: (6 Field Gun positions) commenced.	AR
"	3.		Work as on 2ⁿᵈ continued. Construction of O.P. for Army artillery Bde. in factory chimney at BAC ST MAUR. General overhaul of equipment and repair of wagons, etc.	AR
"	4.		Work as on 3ʳᵈ. Work started on new trenches & FLEURBAIX defences in H.20 21 22 26 27 29.	AR
"	5		Work as on 4 — Site for heavy M.G. Emplacement (tunnels) chosen — FLEURBAIX.	AR

WAR DIARY or INTELLIGENCE SUMMARY

229th Field Coy. R.E.

APRIL 1918.

Place	Date	Hour	Summary of Events and Information	Remarks and references to Appendices
Bac. St. Maur G.13.b.5.6.	April 6		MAP 36. /40.000. Work as on 5. Work on dummy M.G. Emplacements in front of Bac. St. Maur commenced. Camouflage Screens representing Beet Stack with M.G. loophole erected and parts made to them.	O.R.
	7		Work as on 6th. Cork Emergency bridge completed except for camouflage.	O.R.
	8		" " " 7th	O.R.
	9		Enemy Artillery became active during Early morning. Several direct hits obtained	
	5:0 AM		on Coy. H.Q. billets. It was evident that a little bombardment / advance of Enemy Infantry was in progress. The Company was turned out and paraded in fighting order at once. Orders received	
	6:15 AM		from O.C. to Stand to Bridge (for demolition) and the bridges between G.21.d & G.12.a. Orders to run out the Emergency bridge. (post) to fix charges on the permanent Bridge and post Bridge Head Guarding parties during the morning. The remainder of the Company (approx 50 O.R.)	
	2:0 PM		Orders received to move all transport back to Neuf-Berquin.	
	2:0 PM		119th Inf. Bde H.Q. established in field C. H.Q. at Bac. St. Maur G.13.3.5.9. and as the Enemy had by this time reached the South Bank of 178 in several places the 50 O.R. standing by were placed at the disposal of the G.O.C. 119th Inf. Bde. for the defence of the line running through G.18.b.72.	

Army Form C. 2118.

WAR DIARY
or
INTELLIGENCE SUMMARY.

(Erase heading not required.)

22nd Field Coy. RE (3)

APRIL 1918

Place	Date	Hour	Summary of Events and Information	Remarks and references to Appendices
BAC. ST. MAUR	APRIL	MAP. 36 1/40000	The four cork bridges (pont) were destroyed, the permanent bridge at SAILLY-SUR-LA-LYS G.16.b central was successfully blown at 6.0 P.M. The two pontoon bridges adjacent to the permanent bridge were destroyed by hand. The second permanent bridge at G.16.c.8.6. was partially blown at 6.10 P.M. Complete demolition was not secured in this latter bridge and the officer in charge - LIEUT- J.G. VECE, RE. made several efforts to destroy it - with possible changes made up from spare guncotton but owing to defective primers this was unsuccessful. After no more could be done at the Bridges, the Sappers engaged were withdrawn to the strong points on NIEPPE side of the LYS in G.21.b & G.16.a & b thus holding a line conforming to that held by 150 Sappers further north under command of G.O.C. 114 Inf. Bde. Under orders received from C.R.E. at 5.30 P.M. Coy. H.Q. was moved to CUL-DE-SAC FARM G.14.a. Junction with 231 Field Coy. R.E. Patrols (largely made up of stragglers) placed under command of Sapper N.C.O.s) were sent out from CUL-DE-SAC FARM during the night and had obtained with Sappers in posts the Sappers holding the posts were relieved by M2 Royal Scotts Fusiliers and under orders of C.R.E. were withdrawn to Transport	
	10th			

WAR DIARY
INTELLIGENCE SUMMARY

229th Field Coy RE

APRIL 1918.

Place	Date	Hour	Summary of Events and Information	Remarks and references to Appendices
NEUF BERQUIN	10"		Lines at NEUF BERQUIN in STEEN WERCK Suffers who had not been able to regain Coy HQ. at Bac St Maur feed by Pion. Time re-assembled at NEUF BERQUIN except Plos under Lieut. BORRIE, Lt. VOCE & Lieut. EASTON Lt. LESLIE who had became absorbed into various infantry units, holding the front Croix-du-Bac. These remained with infantry holding the line.	
		3.0p.	Orders received to let field Coy. but Transport was to move to MERRIS and Suffers toStand by to Support "114" by Bde. of Regimental Transport moves to MERRIS close to Railway.	
		5.0p.	Definite orders received to move forward (Sappers) to LE VERRIER or Report to G.O.C. 114" Inf. Bde. at that place. Company arrived at LE VERRIER at 7.0 p.m. and deployed to hold LE VERRIER — STEEN WERCK Road astride A 20 central. An attack was developing further orders were given to hold front line and fill the gap between 88" Bde. 29" Div. on left and 9" L.N.L. 25. Division on right to position of three plants being A15 a 5.4 and A 22 a 2.3. An order of battle was 229 Fd.SC.RE Coy. 224 Field Coy centre & 231" Fd.S.C° right. 23" Field Cy. with 9. L.N.L. but it was driven in to its 11" unit Tunnel was immediately detained on the right	NBR

WAR DIARY
or
INTELLIGENCE SUMMARY

Army Form C. 2118.

229 Field C.R.E.

APRIL 1918.

Place	Date	Hour	Summary of Events and Information	Remarks and references to Appendices
LE VERRIER A.15.a.5.A	11		MAP. 36. ⅕₀,₀₀₀	
			Before touch on the left was established with the 1/5" York-Lancs. A9" Division which had been sent up to reinforce 183 Inf. Bde.	
		11.0 a.m.	The right flank had to be withdrawn at 11.0 a.m. to conform to movement of troops entering the further South and there were Divisional R.E. pivoted round on the left flank of 229 field C.R.E. who were still in touch with the 1/5 York the Line held by 15/40 Division R.E. was then approx. NOM to SOUTH 300" EAST of LA BECQUE FARM A 14 b.d.	
		3.0 p.m.	At 3.0 p.m. it was discovered that the troops on the left had disappeared and shortly after the 9th L.N.R. on the right flank reported severe enfilade M.G. fire from the right. It was decided to hold on but at	O.R.
		4.0 p.m.	4.0 p.m. the C.R.E. left flank was heavily enfiladed also and a withdrawal carried out in good order. un made to the road 300" east of LA BECQUE farm.. Casualties were suffered during this movement but all the wounded were got away. On reaching the road further efforts were made to keep in touch with the enemy, pushed forward again to the villas roed to establish touch with the enemy. Efforts were made without success to establish touch on the left	

WAR DIARY or INTELLIGENCE SUMMARY

Army Form C. 2118.

229 Field Coy RE

April 1918

Place	Date	Hour	Summary of Events and Information	Remarks and references to Appendices
La Becque Farm A19.b.0.3	11		At 6.30 p.m. orders were received for OC. details 25 Div. on right that stating that 31st Div. had come into line and was about to counter attack, and that a defensive flank was to be formed by 4 to 40th Div. RE. and 1st 25 Div. details left to rest on FARM at A.9.4.6.2 and its right in copse in A.15.d. this forward line were quickly established and rifle pots dug — H.Q. was SGR H.Q. Line of the 31st Div. The counter attacking from together crossed in front of this line. At 11.0 p.m. to line of posts was taken over by D.L.I. 31st Div. On completion of relief the three companies concentrated and moved to BAILLEUL, billets and trans was moved to farm one mile west of STRAZEELE on STRAZEELE, (PRADELLES Rd.) where transport had been compelled to move when shelled out of lines at MERRIS early in morning. After the concentration referred to above and one section 229 field Coy RE. ordered to formed its movements of to remaining three sections were as follows. Having available Row put our A.Q.9. and obtained front with 11th right post 4 a Br. of 4. Lancashire Fusiliers 25th Div. dug themselves in and proceeded to put the farm in a state of defence	BR

WAR DIARY or INTELLIGENCE SUMMARY

Army Form C. 2118.

229 Field Coy RE

APRIL 1917

Place	Date	Hour	Summary of Events and Information	Remarks and references to Appendices
STRAZEELE	11		The flank guard followed by the main body of RE moved forward and took post and fog tired our East with Pte post on Aga 62. Emergency was relieved by 1st D.L.I. 31st Div. at 11.0 p.m. Such places RE parts did not join the main body. Having ascertained a patrol that the C in C had moved forward it was realised that his farm caused to protect the Capt. Plunk and others, was made to rejoin the main body of RE by moving towards the right along the road held at 6.0 p.m. At dawn on 12 — not knowing the relief and having no orders to withdraw to Senior RE officer placed Cie posts under command of C.O. of a Bn. 4th West Yorks Regt. 31st Div. and remained with the 12 noon during the time here. At this hour word was received that 40' Div. had been withdrawn and arrangements with West Yorks R.E. withdrew and proceeded to CAESTRE via STRAZEELE. The Coy obtained with 40' Div. and information received that transport Cie and CT were at HONDEGHEM while transport proceeded reporting here at 6.0 p.m. The section which had arrived at STRAZEELE at 11.0 a.m. stood by and orders were received at 3.0 p.m. to return to bivouac of STRAZEELE.	

WAR DIARY or INTELLIGENCE SUMMARY

229 Feld C.R.E.

April 1918

Place	Date	Hour	Summary of Events and Information	Remarks and references to Appendices
STRAZEELE	12.	"1.0 a.m 0"	Picks Shovels were obtained and consolidation of line held by a composite Battn of 149 Inf Bde = 121 Inf Bde was proceeded with. The work was carried out in slight drizzle during the night and morning of the 13th by which time a practically continuous line was dug.	
	13	2.0.	Orders received to concentrate on transport lines at HONDEGHEM preparatory to moving out.	
			Orders received at 5.0 h. that see field Cope. Fences &c were under orders of O.C. 229 Field Co. R.E. to strengthen screen at VIEPPE. Cos moved to VIEPPE & remained there during the night.	C.R.E.
			Total Casualties during the operation Killed 3 o.r. Wounded 1 off. 27 o.r. happy since the Wounded 2 Missing 3 o.r. Unaccounted for 6 o.r.	
MEPPE	14.		Cos left MEPPE and marched through St. OMER to CORMETTE. All Field Cos R.E. billeted at CORMETTE.	a.s.R
CORMETTE	15.		Cos resting and refitting CORMETTE as a group.	a.s.R
	16.		Cos in training - Drill Rifle drill etc Musketry. Refitting	a.s.R
	17.		On 16th 3 o.r. unaccounted for turned up at CORMETTE having been with 31st Div.	c.s.R

WAR DIARY
or
INTELLIGENCE SUMMARY.

Army Form C. 2118.

8.
229 Field Co. R.E.

April 1918.

Place	Date	Hour	Summary of Events and Information	Remarks and references to Appendices
CORNETTE	18.		Company together with G.O.C. 40 Division was inspected by tunnels and hauled them for the good work the has done in the River Lys Battle. 204. 24 of all Ranks & 2 wagons transferred to 229 field Co. R.E. to complete their strength to establishment.	ASR
"	19.		Musketry.	ASR
"	20.		Orders received to proceed to PETIT DIFQUES.	ASR
PETIT DIFQUES	21.		Co. march to PETIT DIFQUES a "21".	ACSR
"	22.		Co. in training at PETIT DIFQUES.	ASR
"	23.		- do -	ASR
"	24.		Company moved to ST SYLVESTRE. Personnel by M.T. Bus transport by road. Tents supplied and Company settle down under canvas in field half way between St Sylvestre & St Marie Cassel.	ASR
ST SYLVESTRE	25.		Company employed with 231" field Co. R.E. on digging and camouflaging posts on new defence line W. of St Sylvestre.	ASR
	26.		- do -	ASR

WAR DIARY
or
INTELLIGENCE SUMMARY. (9)

Army Form C. 2118.

APRIL 1918. 229 Labour Coy

Sheet 27 NE. 1/20,000.

Place	Date	Hour	Summary of Events and Information	Remarks and references to Appendices
St. Sylvestre Cappel	27.		Orders received at 12.30 A.M. 27. to move to HERZEELE taking over a defence line between HERZEELE and OUDE ZEELE. Coy. moved to South of HERZEELE and pitched camp in field at D.2.b.4.6. Details 1 Off. - 6 oth - 12 O.R. attached to 66th Div.	GSR
HERZEELE D.2.w.b.4.6.	28.		6 Coy. training in supervision of Chinese labour on new defence line. Two Chinese labour Companies attached to Coy.	
"			Coy. resting. Officers Rifle new outpost line and Buffer line between HERZEELE and OUDE ZEELE. 1 R.E. of 66 Div. attached. 3 Off. 16 O.R. attached. Infantry taken away.	GSR
	29.		Coy. employed on new outpost line between HERZEELE & OUDEZEELE. Running out hedges + taking out the line and for Chinese labourers. Officers [illegible] at Buffer line a rear of outpost line.	GSR
	30.		Coy. employed a new Outpost & Buffer lines. thinning hedges & supervising work of two Chinese labour Companies.	GSR

A Blewin
Capt. O.C.
O.C. 229 Field Coy R.E.

Vol 24

229th FIELD COY. R.E.

WAR DIARY

MAY 1918   Vol. 23

SECRET

Army Form C. 2118.

WAR DIARY
or
INTELLIGENCE SUMMARY.
(Erase heading not required.)

229th FIELD COY. R.E. 40th DIVISION.

Place	Date	Hour	Summary of Events and Information	Remarks and references to Appendices
HERZEELE D.1.A.a.3.4	MAY 1.	SEE APPENDIX "A"	Company with remainder of Divisional Engineers detached from Division and working under CE VII Corps on construction of Rear line of defence between HERZEELE & CASSEL. A system of trenches under construction called the WINNEZEELE LINE consisting of an outpost line and a main defence or battle line about 1000 yards in rear. The original plan of having the outpost line consist of isolated posts concealed behind hedges is altered and its outpost line is to be made a continuous defence line in the same way as the main battle line.	OCR
	2		Company is employing four Chinese labour Companies on construction of these lines between HERZEELE [WORMHOUDT - HOUTKERQUE ROAD] and OUDEZEELE. Considerable difficulty experienced in drainage, huge amount of trench work being to be put up in account of the high permanent water level. Lieut. KNIGHT R.E. 231st Field Co R.E. attached to Company.	OCR
	3		Work as on 1st. A/Sgt. LINTON RE awarded CROIX de GUERRE.	OCR
	4		" " " Lieut. F. HINMAN RE (MW) awarded MILITARY MEDAL.	OCR
			Effective Strength of Company: 7 Officers 183 O.R.	OCR
	5		Work as on 1st including 20 O.R. attached to 22A field C.R.E. returned 2 of 24 O.R. attached to 229 Field Coy R.E. are returned.	OCR
	6		Work as on 1st. New Scheme in front. about 1000 yards taken over from 229 Field Coy R.E.	OCR
	7		Work as on 6th.	OCR

Army Form C. 2118.

WAR DIARY
or
INTELLIGENCE SUMMARY
(Erase heading not required.)

229th FIELD Coy R.E. 46th DIVISION

MAY 1918.

Place	Date	Hour	Summary of Events and Information	Remarks and references to Appendices
HERZEELE D.14.a.3.4.	May 8		Work on line as above + in Appendix A.	QBR
	9		do	QBR
		P.M.	1 Off - 1 O.R. Leave. Co's rejoin 231st Field Co R.E.	
			1 O.R. rejoins from Hospital. 1 Off. + 10 O.R. from 224 Field C.R.E.	
	10		Work on line as above and in Appendix A.	QBR
	11		- do -	
	12		Effective Strength 7 Off. 137 O.R. including 1 Off. 5 O.R. attached 1 O.R. on leave.	QBR
do	13		Work in Outpost Line + Main Line of Resistance carried on as described in Appendix A	
	14		- do -	
	15			
	16			
	17			
	18		1 O.R. on leave. Effective Strength 7 Off. 135 O.R. with 1 Off. 3 O.R. detached	QBR
	19		Work as on 11th	QBR
	20		15 O.R. of M.G. positions held + attached with Six Emmy Gms	G.P.R.
			Transport of R.E. Stores. 2 O.R. attached from 126 H.B.I.C. H.Q. for instruction in Carpentering	QBR
	21		Work as on 11th	

WAR DIARY
INTELLIGENCE SUMMARY

229 Field Coy R.E. 40th Div.

MAY 1918

Army Form C. 2118.

Place	Date	Hour	Summary of Events and Information	Remarks and references to Appendices
HERZEELE D.19.a.3.4.	May 22		Work on WINNEZEELE Line as in Appendix A.	ASR
	23.		-do- A/Sgt. LINTON, Spr. DRAKE awarded the MILITARY MEDAL for gallantry during operations April 9-13.	ASR
	24		Work as above. Effective Strength 7 off. 185 O.R. incl. 1 off. + 4 O.R. detached. 1 O.R. on leave.	ASR
	25			ASR
	26.		1 O.R. granted leave.	ASR
	27		Work as above.	ASR
	28			ASR
	29.		C.S.M. THIRLWALL awarded Distinguished Conduct Medal for gallantry during operations April 9-13.	ASR
	30		Work as in appendix A.	
	31			ASR

A.Dunkl
C/P Ridgewell
229

Army Form C. 2118.

WAR DIARY
or
INTELLIGENCE SUMMARY.
(Erase heading not required.)

APPENDIX A.

229th Field Coy. R.E. 40th Div

MAY 1918.

Place	Date	Hour	Summary of Events and Information	Remarks and references to Appendices
WINNEZEELE LINE.			During May the Company has been employed continuously on the WINNEZEELE LINE. During May four Chinese Labour Companies attached – 53½ = 66⅓ : 175 =132. **Defence System** The original scheme of defence was to have a Main line of Resistance consisting of a continuous fire trench and about 1000 yds. in front an Outpost line consisting of isolated posts dug behind hedges or other cover and carefully camouflaged. Dimensions and selection of posts being such that they could either be connected up into a continuous line or the scheme was subsequently extended so that the system now comprises :- 1. Outpost Line. A continuous fire trench as carefully concealed as possible. 2. A Main Line of Resistance a continuous fire trench 500 yds. (approx.) behind the Outpost Line with a Support line 200 yds in rear. 3. A Reserve Line a continuous fire trench 1000 yds (approx) behind Main Line with a Support trench 200 ft in rear. All lines to be wired with low wire entanglement or single apron fence. TRACE All trenches to be of following trace (Fig.i) Fig.i TYPICAL SECTION IN DRY GROUND. Fig.ii	

WAR DIARY
INTELLIGENCE SUMMARY. APPENDIX A (2)

MODIFICATION OF SECTION IN WET GROUND

Where the water level was less than 3'-0" from the surface the typical section given in fig.ii was modified so that the bottom of the trench was kept about 6" to 1'-6" above water level. The parapet was built correspondingly high to give the standard 4'-6" protection. Where the water level was on or very close to ground level Breastworks were erected, eliminating sheer gravel. Being kept nearly in front of trench as shown in fig.iii.

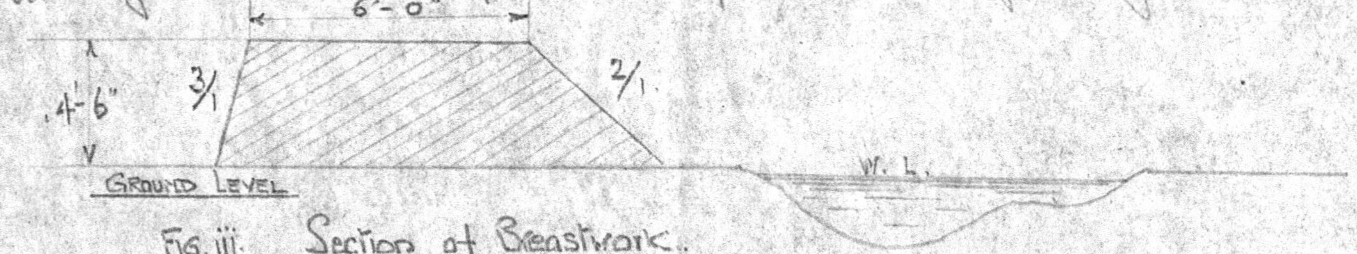

Fig. iii. Section of Breastwork.

Where trenches had been dug to depth of 3'-0" during dry weather and subsequent rain raised that level over (?) the trench was modified as shown in fig.iv.

AAA — original trench.
(B) BB — modified trench.

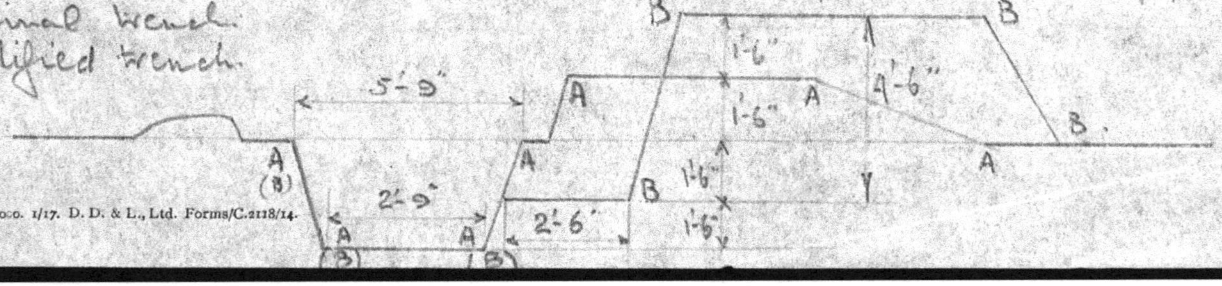

Fig. IV.

Army Form C. 2118.

WAR DIARY
or
INTELLIGENCE SUMMARY. APPENDIX A (3)
(Erase heading not required.)

Place	Date	Hour	Summary of Events and Information	Remarks and references to Appendices
			DRAINAGE. When work was first commenced the weather was fairly dry, but about the 3rd of the month there was heavy rainfall and considerable difficulty was experienced with drainage. The trenches had been connected by short open cuts to the existing canal drains but these did not take away all the water. They were choked up and soon became flooded. Consequently a large amount of labour was turned on to clearing and deepening these canal drains and in places digging new ones. By this means a flow of water was obtained and in about five days time this had completely cleared the trenches except in the very low lying parts where the trenches had to be modified as in fig. iv. Particular stress was laid on the necessity for camouflage. **CAMOUFLAGE.** The trenches and lightly then this was screened in the first place by sticking them wherever possible behind hedges. At the same time attention was paid to obtaining planting fire and trees used to cross a stretch of open ground in general where a about 200 yds. in rear from obscuring the position of the removed earth part and at the same time from giving good planting fig. wherever trenches were dug in grain bearing the soil, were removed – not only from the site of the trench itself but from the points	

WAR DIARY
or
INTELLIGENCE SUMMARY.   APPENDIX A.

Army Form C. 2118.

In front where the parapet was to be formed. After observing it the parapet & panacks were completed covering up loop holes.

HEDGES. Where trenches were dug behind hedges the hedges cut as a rule to be thinned out in part, to give a clear view forwards. The tops of hedges however were left untouched wherever possible to afford concealment from above. the hedges so thinned were then wired up.

Employment of Chinese labour.

Of the four Chinese Coys. employed, two had been in trenches some months working on dumps and the remaining two had just landed. None had had any trench digging experience. It was found necessary to organise the supervision of the inexperienced labour very carefully, the scheme adopted being to place one Sapper in charge of a small body of coolies to be responsible for the technical execution of the work. The Sappers as far as possible gave their instructions through to their M.C.Os attached to Chinese labour Companies.

A task work system was adopted throughout as it was found that the Chinese worked very much better in that way.

Army Form C. 2118.

WAR DIARY
or
INTELLIGENCE SUMMARY.   APPENDIX A. (5)
(Erase heading not required.)

Instructions regarding War Diaries and Intelligence Summaries are contained in F. S. Regs., Part II. and the Staff Manual respectively. Title pages will be prepared in manuscript.

Place	Date	Hour	Summary of Events and Information	Remarks and references to Appendices
			essential to set the maximum tasks as early as possible the coolies would then adopt it as a standard and be satisfied with it. However it was necessary to alter tasks and increase them one day great trouble ensued. Coolies frequently altered its marking tape if very strict supervision was not maintained. Many coolies shewed considerable skill in sod revetting and hedge trimming with shovels after a little practice and the native gangers quickly grasped the essential features of the Gauging only a line of trenches. Wiring. The wiring of all emp. on the Northern Sector was undertaken by D. 231. assisted Coy R.E. with assistance for Chinese labour. Material was supplied by 229 Tun: Coy R.E.	

31.5.17.

CBarrie
Captain R.E.
229 Tun: Coy R.E.

WR 25

229th FIELD COMPANY R.E.

June 1918

Vol 25

War Diary

WAR DIARY or INTELLIGENCE SUMMARY

Army Form C. 2118.

229TH FIELD COY. R.E. 40TH DIVISION

JUNE 1918.

MAP. FRANCE & BELGIUM. SHEET 27. 1/40,000.

Place	Date	Hour	Summary of Events and Information	Remarks and references to Appendices
HERZEELE. D.14.a.3.4.	JUNE 1		Company in Camp near HERZEELE working on the WINNEZEELE LINE – a rear defence line between HERZEELE and CASSEL. Two Chinese companies providing labour for digging trenches, clearing drains, trimming hedges and wiring. Effective Strength of Unit for week ending June 1st: Attached 7 off. 185 OR. 1 off. 22 OR. including Camp Chaplain. – 2 OR detached and 2 on leave to U.K.	WBR
	2		The work on the WINNEZEELE LINE Coy approaching completion, this Section ordered to proceed to ERSKELBRUGGE to commence work on the BALEMBERG LINE. Two Sections and one Chinese Labour Coy. left for WINNEZEELE LINE to complete the communication trenches and the wiring for detail of this work see Appendix A.	WBR. App A.
ERSKELBRUGGE. B.25.b.5.4.	3		Coy H.Q and two sections proceeded by advance party to ERSKELBRUGGE and fitted camp at B.25.b.5.4. One Chinese Labour Coy also moved to same neighbourhood for work on the new LINE. Officers reconnoitre Main LINE of new system and lay out work for the morning. No particular difficulties were encountered for detail of work on BALEMBERG LINE See Appendix B.	WBR. App B.
	4		Work commenced on the BALEMBERG LINE.	
	5		MAJOR F.W. CLARK, R.E. OC 229 FIELDCoy RE. takes over duties of CRE. 40 Div.	
	6 7 8		Work continued on the BALEMBERG LINE. Work carried out as described in Appendix B. Effective Strength of Unit for week ending June 8th 1918. Attached 7 off. 189 OR including 1 off. 3 OR detached. 1 OR on leave.	App B

Army Form C. 2118.

WAR DIARY
or
INTELLIGENCE SUMMARY.

229th FIELD COY R.E. ② 40 DIV.

(Erase heading not required.)

Place	Date	Hour	Summary of Events and Information	Remarks and references to Appendices
ERSKELBRUGGE. B.25.b.5.4.	June 9th	✱	A new Chinese labour Coy attached for work on BALENBERG LINE. Work as in Appendix B. for work see Appendix B.	App.
	10			O.R.R
	11		Two Sections left at HERZEELE having finished Communication trenches, and marking of lines and erection of Elementary belts of Wire are ordered to rejoin the Company at ESKELBRUGGE the Chinese Labour Coy working on the BALENBERG LINE also proceed at same area for work on the BALENBERG LINE.	App. A.
	12			
	13			
	14		Work carried out as described in Appendix B.	O.R.R.
	15			
			Major F.W. CLARK, R.E. resumes command of the Company on its appointment of R.P. PACKENHAM-WALSH. R.E. as C.R.E. 40th DIVISION. Effective Strength of Unit for week ending June 15th 1918. 7 off. 184 O.R.	O.R.R.
✱ June 9th			One Officer including 1 off 3 8 O.R. detached and 2 O.R. on leave and 5 O.R. detailed for work with VII Corps Labor Officer on construct dams for local reserveoirs on the streams in the CASSEL area.	O.R.R.
	16			
	17			
	18			
	19		Work carried out as described in Appendix. B.	O.R.R.
	20			
	21			
	22		Effective Strength of Unit for week ending June 22nd 1918. Attached 7 off 188 O.R. including 10 O.R. detached 1 off + 2 O.R. on leave to U.K. 1 off 33 O.R.	
	23		Work on BALENBER LINE handed over to 236 A.T. Coy R.E. Company proceeds by march route to SERCUS and takes over work on the	App.

WAR DIARY or INTELLIGENCE SUMMARY

Army Form C. 2118.

229th Field Coy R.E. 40' Division

JUNE 1918.

Place	Date	Hour	Summary of Events and Information	Remarks and references to Appendices
SERCUS E.23.d.8.1	Jun 23		MAP FRANCE Sheet 36B 1/40,000 WEST HAZEBROUCK LINE from 236 AT Coy RE Appendix C.	GSR
	24		Work commenced on WEST HAZEBROUCK LINE. Scheme handed over to 236 Field Coy RE. Orders received detailing action of Field Coy in event of enemy attack on the Sector immediately in Front. Company to concentrate in filling order with other Field Cos & A.T. Coys R.E. at U.20.c. to form Mobile Reserve in the West Hazebrouck Line.	GSR
	25 26 27 28		Work continued on the WEST HAZEBROUCK LINE as detailed in Appendix C. Practice Mobilization called for assembly of R.E. units in the Division in case of enemy attack. Company assembled in M.D. U.20.c.— assembly positions allotted to each group of Companies and all officers & men instructed in preliminary duties.	GSR GSR
	29		Work continued on WEST HAZEBROUCK LINE as detailed in Appendix C. Effective Strength of Unit for week ending June 29, 1918. Attached 7 Off. 173 O.R. including 9 O.R. detailed as 1 Off. 2 O.R. or less.	GSR
	30.		Work commenced on Rifle Range for Divisional Troops. No work carried out on Live Company training.	GSR

O.B. Rayner.
Capt. R.E.
for O.C. 229 Field Coy R.E.

APPENDIX A.

WAR DIARY. JUNE 1918. 229TH FIELD COY. R.E.

WORK ON WINNEZEELE.

The work on this sector being well advanced by the End of May and other lines of importance requiring immediate and finished attention by the Company and one Chinese Labour Coy. was left to complete the Communication Trenches and finish the elementary belts of wiring.

The Communication Trenches between the various lines of the system were all sited and strong so near that tendered to be used as Switch line in the event of any line being overrun by the Enemy, to this end they were all dug of a pattern generally orientated as the fire trenches is as under:—

[Cross-section diagrams showing trench dimensions: 20', approx 12', 40', 5'-6", 6", 6'-0", 1'-6", 3'-0", 2'-9"]

The wiring consisted of elementary belts of single apron fence in front of such lines to protect being to splice up features when intervals and laterals are available.

This work was completed on June 10th 1918.

The whole system was marked by advanced pickets — a distinct allowance for each line of the system and also for the Communication Trenches.

June 30th 1918.

O.B.Raynes. Capt R.E.
for O.C. 229th Field Coy R.E.

APPENDIX B.

WAR DIARY. JUNE 1918. 229TH FIELD Coy. RE.

WORK ON BALEMBERG LINE.

On June 3rd Two Sections of the Company and one Chinese labour Coy were moved from HERZEELE to ERSKELBROGGE to start work on the Northern Sector of the BALEMBERG LINE. This line runs from B.13 b north of ERSKELBROGGE through ROEBRUCK H.8 d to BALEMBERG H.27 d southwards.

General

Three Line System.

(1) An outpost or observation line consisting of isolated lengths of trench of standard trace sited behind hedges where possible and so arranged that it can be connected up ultimately into a continuous fire trench if so desired.

(2) A Main Line of Resistance approx 500 yds. behind the observation line. A continuous fire trench of standard trace plan below. Sited where cover positive behind hedges.

(3) A Reserve Line approx. 1000 yds behind Main Line and similar to it in trace & site.

Communication trenches between the various lines sited so that they can be used as suitable trenches if necessary. Of same trace as Main Line.

Wire to be put up in front of each line. (No wire was yet put up in front, but to be implemented by wiring available. Wire staked.)

General Trace of Trench.

※ Trench dug 18" deep regardless of presence of water to give shelter in emergency.

SECTION IN NORMAL GROUND

SECTION OF BREASTWORK IN WATERLOGGED GROUND

APPENDIX B. Cont'd

Where work was started on this line the weather has been very dry for many weeks and in consequence the water level had been considerably lowered below the normal and confirmed by the inhabitants who said that to ascertain by examination of ditches, drains and wells to come to very many years.

Consequently it was decided not to bring the trenches to a greater depth than 18 inches except in very special cases, and wherever the ground was particularly low to build breastworks 4'-6" high. This course was subsequently gratified.

No special difficulties were encountered in this line.

Note on Employment of Chinese Labour

It was found that if the some trouble was taken by the R.E. Supervisor to make the work interesting to the coolie — by allowing him how to do neat sod revetting — to careful covering of parapets in dressing with sods — the trimming of trenches — maintaining a correct batter etc. etc. — he worked far more cheerfully and would get through a much bigger task in shorter time and do very much better work. This we experienced with great success in this line, and was productive of considerable rivalry between various platoons of coolies with excellent results.

June 30th 1915.

[signature]
Capt. R.E.
229 Field Coy.

APPENDIX C

WAR DIARY. JUNE 1918. 229th FIELD COY. R.E.

WORK ON WEST HAZEBROUCK LINE.

Work on this Line taken over from 236' F.T. Co R.E. The trenches were already dug and belts of wire erected. Work to be done as under:-

① Thickening of Main Belt of wire to 45 yds and erection of new belt of similar dimensions 50 yds in front. Provision of sufficient Chevaux de Frise to stretch all roads (Subject of Arg'ts at once last June.

② Clearing of Crops in front of trench to give clear view of ranges. (Subsequently field up kept in arrangements with French Authorities).

③ Revetting of trench. Started with Brushwood hurdle made on site laid in place & pickets driven in - wired back.

④ Draining of Line. Drain was already dug but required cementing up. the parapets, this was done by making a covered brushwood drain in Sketch.

⑤ Provision of O.P.s & M.G. Emplacements.

This work was started but very little was possible before end of month owing to difficulty in obtaining material.

[sketch showing trench cross-section with "3' Pickets" and "Brushwood Hurdle"]

June 30. 1918.

O.S.Campbell. Capt. R.E.
O.C. 229th Field Coy R.E.

WR 26

JULY 1918

WAR DIARY

229th FIELD Coy. R.E.

VOL 26

Army Form C. 2118.

WAR DIARY or INTELLIGENCE SUMMARY.
(Erase heading not required.)

229TH FIELD COY R.E. 40TH DIVISION.

Reference Map. FRANCE. Sheet 36A. 1/40,000

July 1918.

Place	Date	Hour	Summary of Events and Information	Remarks and references to Appendices
SERCUS C.3.d.8.1.	July 1st		Company in Camp at SERCUS C.3.d.8.1. The Company is employed on the construction and improvement of the WEST HAZEBROUCK LINE between V.25 central (Map France Sheet 27 1/40,000) and C.12 & 9.3 Sheet 36A. and is also engaged in construction of Rifle Ranges for the 40th Division. For details of work, schemes etc. see Appendix A.	AA
	2nd		Work on WEST HAZEBROUCK LINE as described in Appendix A. Construction of Rifle Range for 40th Division at LE NOIR TROU U.26.a.4.6. One Section employed thereon.	AA
	3rd		Work on WEST HAZEBROUCK LINE and on Rifle Range as on 2nd.	AA
	4th		do.	AA
	5th		do.	AA
	6th		do.	AA
	7th		Company inspected on parade by C.R.E. 40th Division at 10.30 a.m. followed by drill and technical training. Effective Strength of Unit for week ending July 6th 1918. 7 Offrs. 177 OR. including 1 Offr. & 7 OR. detached.	AA
	8th		Work on WEST HAZEBROUCK LINE & on Rifle Range as on 2nd. See Appendix A.	AA

Army Form C. 2118.

WAR DIARY or INTELLIGENCE SUMMARY.

(Erase heading not required.)

229th FIELD Coy. R.E. 40th DIVISION

Instructions regarding War Diaries and Intelligence Summaries are contained in F. S. Regs., Part II. and the Staff Manual respectively. Title pages will be prepared in manuscript.

JULY 1918.

Place	Date	Hour	Summary of Events and Information	Remarks and references to Appendices
	JULY		MAP. FRANCE Sheets. 27 & 36a. 1/40.000.	
SERCUS	9th		Work on WEST HAZEBROUCK line and on Rifle Range as on 2nd Inst.	A.R.
C.3.d.8.1.	10		do	A.R.
"	11		do	A.R.
"	12		do	A.R.
"	13		do	A.R.
			Orders received to take over work on WEST HAZEBROUCK Line to South of where Company had been working. The new Sector runs from original Left boundary in V.25 central Range Old right boundary in C.12.c. to D.25.c. Central. This Sector was taken over from 173 Tunnelling Coy. R.E. Orders received later to take over work on the ROMARIN defence C.17.d, 18.c, 24.a, from the 554 A.T. Coy. R.E.	A.R.
"	14		No work on defence. Company in training. Drill, musketry etc.	A.R.
"	15		Work on new Sector allotted to Sections and work commenced. House taken Companies employed. For detail of work see Appendix B. Effective Strength for week ending July 13th 7 off. 187 O.R. incl 1 off. 8 O.R. detached.	A.R.
"	16		Work on WEST HAZEBROUCK Line & Rifle Range as on 15th. No work attempted on ROMARIN defence owing to shortage of labour and the amount of important work on the WEST HAZEBROUCK Line.	A.R.

Army Form C. 2118.

WAR DIARY
or
INTELLIGENCE SUMMARY.

(Erase heading not required.)

229TH FIELD Coy R.E. 40TH DIVISION

JULY 1918.

MAPS. FRANCE SHEETS 27 & 36 ¹/₄₀,₀₀₀

Place	Date	Hour	Summary of Events and Information	Remarks and references to Appendices
SERCUS. C.3.d.8.1.	JULY 17.		Work on WEST HAZEBROUCK LINE & on Rifle Range as on 16. Heavy rain flooded many trenches in which it had not been possible to complete its clearance before drawing up on taking over the Sector. Original drains were not so deep as the trench & so were useless. A large amount of the labour was therefore concentrated on this work. Difficulty also experienced on the Rifle Range due to expansion of the clay at the backs of Markers Trench facing up the bottom and breaking struts. This was due to a seam just sand being struck.	a/s/r
	18		Work as on 17	O.R.R.
	19		— do —	O.R.R.
	20		— do —	O.R.R.
	21		No work on defences. Divisional R.E. Sports held.	O.R.R.
	22		Effective Strength 7 offrs. 156 O.R. (incl. 6 O.R. detached S.2.ft. 1 O.R. on leave) Work on West Hazebrouck Line as on 17. An additional Labour Coy attached for work. (No 94)	O.R.R.
	23		— do —	
	24		— do —	
	25		— do —	

Army Form C. 2118.

WAR DIARY
or
INTELLIGENCE SUMMARY.

(Erase heading not required.)

229TH FIELD Coy. R.E. 40TH Division (4)

Title pages July 1918.

Place	Date	Hour	Summary of Events and Information	Remarks and references to Appendices
SERCUS	July 26.	MAP. FRANCE. Sheet 27 & 36. A. 40.000.	Work on WEST HAZEBROUCK LINE continued as described in Appendix B.	A.
C.3.d.8.1.	27		do	A.& B.
	28		No work on defences. Work on Rifle Range. Remainder of Company in training.	A. & B.
			Effective Strength of Unit for week ending July 27. 7 Off. 203 O.R. held 21 detached. 1 Off. 10 O.R. at least.	A.2.
	29		Work on WEST HAZEBROUCK LINE as on 26. Work on new Rifle Range commenced. C.2.2.c.	A.2.
	30		do	A.2.
	31		do	B.B.

O.B.Rayle
Capt. R.E.
for O.C. 229th Field Coy. R.E.

H.Q.
229TH FIELD COY.,
R.E.
No.........................
Date 31.7.18.

Army Form C. 2118.

APPENDIX "A"

WAR DIARY
or
INTELLIGENCE SUMMARY.

(Erase heading not required.)

Instructions regarding War Diaries and Intelligence Summaries are contained in F. S. Regs., Part II. and the Staff Manual respectively. Title pages will be prepared in manuscript.

Place	Date	Hour	Summary of Events and Information	Remarks and references to Appendices

APPENDIX "A". Work on WEST HAZEBROUCK LINE from Y25 central (Sheet 27) - C12a (Sh. 36°) 1.7.18 - 13.7.18

This Line as taken over during the latter part of June 1918 consisted of a Main Line with Support and Reserve Line and in places element of an Outpost Line. The drainage system was bad - the trenches particularly when dug in clay were weathering badly. This necessitated a complete new drainage scheme being evolved and considerable labour being devoted to revetting the trenches. Work is first line a "fighting line". The details of work is described below.

TRENCHES. FRONT LINE or MAIN LINE (sometimes called the "Z" Line). This Line has been drained throughout during the month, all drains being cut through to surface level. The trench has been cleared, parapets thickened until bullet proof, and the interior slopes and in places the back also of the trench revetted with brushwood hurdles made of material found on the site. This in particular required in the Bois de Nor Puits C12a2c.

SUPPORT LINE. Work of a similar nature has been done on Main Line has been carried out all through.

RESERVE LINE. Work is required as on Main Line. O Line has been done but labour was available to complete.

COMMUNICATION TRENCHES. Communication trenches drained and cleared.

Army Form C. 2118.

WAR DIARY
or
INTELLIGENCE SUMMARY.
(Erase heading not required.)

Instructions regarding War Diaries and Intelligence Summaries are contained in F. S. Regs., Part II, and the Staff Manual respectively. Title pages will be prepared in manuscript.

Place	Date	Hour	Summary of Events and Information	Remarks and references to Appendices
			APPENDIX "A" Cont'd.	
M.G. Emplacements			It was at first intended to 6 feet Concrete M.G. Emplacements on the line but the scheme was cancelled and all M.G.'s constructed as open positions in pairs. Particular attention was paid to camouflaging all work & to avoiding making of track to site.	
O.P.			Several protected O.P.'s constructed in front line.	
WIRE.			MAIN LINE. Belt of wire 70' thick was complete in this Sector including over. Chevaux de Frise included constructed for blocking all roads.
OUTPOST LINE. A double Apron fence was erected along whole front of Outpost line.
SUPPORT LINE. Scheme. To erect a 35 ft belt along Support Line. This is 75% finished.	
CROPS.			All crops within 250 yds of Main Line (forwards only) were cut down to give clear field of fire. Arrangements for this were made thro' to French Mission.	

Army Form C. 2118.

APPENDIX "B" WAR DIARY or INTELLIGENCE SUMMARY.

(Erase heading not required.)

Place	Date	Hour	Summary of Events and Information	Remarks and references to Appendices
APPENDIX "B"			Work on WEST HAZEBROUCK LINE V.25 central — D.25.c.	

The new Sector of the West Hazebrouck Line was taken over on July 13, 1918 from 16/173 Tunnelling Coy R.E. It consists of a Main Line Support Line (incomplete in places) and Reserve Line with Communication Trenches. The first line was to be deepened to 6'-0" and revetted with A Frames, the 2nd to be done as a considerable part during the dry weather preceded its hand over and chain had been deepened to correspond. Consequently wire (trestle wocks 6ot in April 18) Entanglements were floated and still not taken had to be dried. Dts drainage scheme where had been drawn up & put into operation on taking over.

Very little work and no wiring had been done on the Support Reserve Lines. C.T. also had not been Duckboarded for a considerable Dist. Consequently a large amount of work after taking over was devoted to trench repairs until a line so plan shield could stand the weather. Work on M.G. Gun Cutting winning was also carried on.

TRENCHES. MAIN LINE. Chief work during month. Drainage. The whole front was carefully cleared and trenches graded. A reasonably dry line was eventually obtained Revetting. Completion of revetting with A Frames where trench had been deepened.

WAR DIARY
or
INTELLIGENCE SUMMARY.
(Erase heading not required.)

Army Form C. 2118.

Place	Date	Hour	Summary of Events and Information	Remarks and references to Appendices
			In one place where trench dug in clay had been deepened to 6'0" in dry weather and not revetted, the whole trench fell in during the first day or two of wet weather, causing a large expenditure of labour to dig it out again and revet. This shews the necessity for immediately revetting wire trench and clay, and also for a general change of scheme to be carried out before or immediately after the digging of the trench.	
SUPPORT LINE:			A certain amount of work was carried out on the line. Principal revetting & draining. Trenches connected up in places.	
C.T.s			These were cleaned & drained. New C.T.s dug where required to give ample communication between front & support line.	
WIRE.			A 40' belt was completed in the centre in front line on taking over. Wire on Support line commenced & 40% completed out 35 ft belt.	
M.G.s			Open M.G. Emplacements in pairs carefully camouflaged (one during and after work).	
CROPS.			All crops for 250 yds in front of Main Line were cut down & all crops between trench and wire in Support Line also.	

WAR DIARY
or
INTELLIGENCE SUMMARY.

Army Form C. 2118.

Place	Date	Hour	Summary of Events and Information	Remarks and references to Appendices
			Scheme for demolition of Houses. A scheme for demolition in event of the Main Line was prepared. All houses which would interfere with view or with fire and which would arise Enemy approach were included.	
Nesle & Labour			Few (white) labour Companies were employed on this line. The Scheme of employment was to indicate to work & explain details to the Labour Coy Officers & NCO's and leave a minimum number of Sappers in supervisory duty.	

31-7-18

O Blayne
Capt RE
f/o C.R.E. 2nd Inf Bde CRE

WAR DIARY.

229th FIELD COMPANY R.E.

Vol. 24

August 1918

WAR DIARY or INTELLIGENCE SUMMARY.

Army Form C. 2118.

229th FIELD Co. R.E. 40th DIVISION

AUGUST 1918.

MAP: FRANCE. SHEET 36ª /40000.

Place	Date	Hour	Summary of Events and Information	Remarks and references to Appendices
SERCUS C.3.d.1.8.	1st		Company employed on construction of WEST HAZEBROUCK line. For details of work carried out on this line see Appendix A.	OR
	2		Company in Camp near SERCUS. Part of one section employed on construction of Rifle Range for the 40th Division. Work on W. HAZEBROUCK line as in Apx A.	OR
	3		— do — — do —	OR
			Effective Strength Unit for week ending 3.8.18. Officers 7. OR. 202 held Detached 2 or leave 10.	
	4		Work on W. HAZEBROUCK LINE as on 2nd.	OR
	5		— do — — do —	OR
	6		— do — — do —	OR
	7		— do — — do —	OR
	8		— do — — do —	OR
	9		— do — — do —	OR
	10		— do — — do —	OR
	11		— do — — do —. One Officer detailed to attend to King's Inspection.	OR
			Effective Strength for week ending 11-8-18. Officers 7. OR. 201 held Detached 4 of leave 2.	OR

Army Form C. 2118.

WAR DIARY
or
INTELLIGENCE SUMMARY.

229th FIELD COY R.E. 40th Division.

(Erase heading not required.)

AUGUST 1918.

MAP. FRANCE SHEET 36A./40,000.

Place	Date	Hour	Summary of Events and Information	Remarks and references to Appendices
SERCUS	12		Work on WEST HAZEBROUCK LINE as in Appendix A. Work ceased on Ranges	app R
C.3.d.1.8.	13		do	app R
"	14		do	app R
"	15		do	app R
"	16		do	app R
"	17		Effective Strength of Unit for week ending 17.8.18. Officers 7. o.r. 204. held. detached 9 o.r. Leave 1 o.r.	app R
"	18		Work on WEST HAZEBROUCK LINE as in Appendix A.	app R
"	19		do	app R
"	20		do	app R
"	21		do	app R
"	22		Work on War Hazebrouck line ceases preparating to movement on 23rd into the new Divisional Area in VIEUX BERQUIN Sector. Work n/t handed over to any other unit.	app R
HAZEBROUCK	23		Company proceed by march route into new area relieving 223rd FIELD Coy R.E.	app R
D.9.b.5.4.			31st Division in RIGHT Sector of DIVISIONAL line. Work handed over	
			1 O.R. 223 FCoRE. Chief work taken over was:—	

WAR DIARY or INTELLIGENCE SUMMARY

Army Form C. 2118.

229th FIELD Coy. R.E. 40TH DIVISION

AUGUST 1918.

Place	Date	Hour	Summary of Events and Information	Remarks and references to Appendices
HAZEBROUCK D.9.b.5.4.	23.		MAP FRANCE. SHEET 36 c/40,000. Maintenance and daily testing of leads & charges laid in position for demolition of bridges and roads in Rigor Sector.	A.B.
"	24.		Owing to the great distance of the Company billets taken over, from Kiels four Sections were moved up to LA MOTTE & surrounded billets.	C.D.
"	25.		Coy. H.Q. moved to LA MOTTE.	E.F.
			LA MOTTE Demolitions. Work: Maintenance & testing of charges for Pont de Prery and VIEUX BERQUIN: Construction of bridge over stream.	
"	26		Work as on 25th.	all
"	27		" " "	
"	28		" " " . Works Company attached from 119th Inf. Bde.	all
"	29		Work as on 28. Works Coy. Employed on road repairs.	all
"	30		Enemy reported to have retired for his position opposite our front. Roads in front of Divisional line reconnoitred. Section & Work Coy Employed on pushing forward roads into & in front of VIEUX BERQUIN	all
"	31.		All work concentrated on roads in front of VIEUX BERQUIN - completion of bridge.	all

Major R.E.
O.C. 229th Field Coy. R.E.

Army Form C. 2118.

WAR DIARY
or
INTELLIGENCE SUMMARY.
(Erase heading not required.)

229 Field Coy R.E.

Place	Date	Hour	Summary of Events and Information	Remarks and references to Appendices
	August 1918.		APPENDIX A.	

WORK ON WEST HAZEBROUCK LINE.

Work on the system continued on same lines as during previous month with the exception that all the Labour Companies personnel employed were taken away and replaced by three Companies of the Divisional Pioneers. These Pioneer Companies were given sectors & the work was explained in detail. The Companies then carried out the work under the supervision & direction of their own officers.

Nature of work.

Work was carried out on the Reserve Line of the System — the Main or "Z" Line, the Support Line and the Reserve Line with their intermediate Communication Trenches, also a wiring & construction of Machine Gun Emplacements.

I. Main Line.

This line was dug throughout and cleared for the greater part during the preceding month. Chief work during August: draining of remainder of line; deepening to 7'0" in the shallow parts, & framing and revetting with hurdles where ground had given way. Also making out to line with Mice Bonds.

Cutting of crops in front of line to distance of 250 yds. completed.

II. Support Line.

Chief work. Clearing out & revetting where fallen in, deepening to 3'0", draining trench. Levelling and reducing parapets where necessary.

III. Reserve Line.

The amount of Labour available did not admit of much work being done on this.

WAR DIARY or INTELLIGENCE SUMMARY

Army Form C. 2118.

Place: Line

Date / Hour: —

Summary of Events and Information: APPENDIX A.

In parts where work could be started clearing, draining and parapet work was carried out.

COMMUNICATION TRENCHES. Two new Communication Trenches were dug between the Main & the Support line to give increased facilities for passage between the two lines. Other C.T.s were deepened, drained and ramped down at forward end to the 7'·0" level of Main line.

WIRING. Wiring on Support and Reserve lines was continued on same lines as hitherto, a belt 35 ft wide was put down in front of Reel trench, the belt being attended by two apron fences & filled in with Highwind Entanglement.

M.G. Emplacements. The construction of M.G. Emplacements was pushed on both in and in front of their line and in Reserve Positions. All emplacements were open - cheese forms isolated from the trenches and well camouflaged from both front and overhead observation.

Finally when the Division moved into the line & the River Defence Sector the work on the Warehead Line was started.

A.Stanger Caple
Major CRE.

WR 28

War Diary

229th Field Company R.E.

Vol. – 28

September 1918.

SECRET

WAR DIARY or INTELLIGENCE SUMMARY

Army Form C. 2118.

229th FIELD Coy. R.E. 40th DIVISION

SEPTEMBER 1918

MAP. FRANCE Sheets 36A & 36. /40,000

Place	Date	Hour	Summary of Events and Information	Remarks and references to Appendices
LA MOTTE D.30.d.14	1st		3 Sections and attached Infantry employed on repair of VIEUX BERQUIN - LE VERRIER Road. This road was left in very good condition except at one point - Hte MAISON 36A/F.14.d.22 where it was Cross stream. This point had been heavily shelled by our artillery & was badly cut up and waterlogged. Large stone dumps were found in various places along the road which great assisted work - some of these dumps were of old British & some of German origin.	
			Three Sections & Work Coy. more into billets in VIEUX BERQUIN.	O.R.
VIEUX BERQUIN 36A/E.24.b.28	2nd		Owing to rapid advance section & Work Cy. again were employed to LE VERRIER F.21.9.80. Work on roads between LE VERRIER DOULIEU & LE VERRIER - STEENWERCK. 8 Coy. HQ. Transport move to VIEUX BERQUIN. 36.	O.R.
			One Section moved forward to A.28.b. & Starts work on bridge at A.29.a.45 over STEEN BECQUE to connect up existing tracks for cruiser traffic.	
LE VERRIER A 36A/F.29.a.80	3rd		Work as on 2nd continued. Work commenced on Second bridge over STEEN BECK at 36/A.29.a.2.4. Coy HQ. Transport move to LE VERRIER	O.R.

Army Form C. 2118.

WAR DIARY
or
INTELLIGENCE SUMMARY.   229TH FIELD COY. R.E. 40 Div.

(Erase heading not required.)

Title pages SEPTEMBER 1918.

Place	Date	Hour	Summary of Events and Information	Remarks and references to Appendices
			MAP — FRANCE Sheet 36 / 10,000.	
LE VERRIER 36c/F.24.c.8.9.	4		Coy employed on Roads & Bridges in DOULIEU area.	CRE
	5.		Bridges as on 3rd. Bridge over STEENBECK at A.29.a.4.8. and A.29.a.2.4. completed. Work on road — 2 Sections and Works Coy. repairing road from DOULIEU v. CROIX NEUF BERQUIN. Bridge over STEENBECK at 36/A.23.d.9.0. Started & completed (DIPPER BRIDGE) gives access to Road to CROIX du BAC & BAC ST MAUR. Bridge erected over stream est DOULIEU ESTAIRES road. Constructed to carry tanks.	CRE
	6.		Bridge in DOULIEU completed. Section's Work CP employed on Road repair and collection of Timber to form dump for future operations.	CRE
LE PETIT MORTIER 36c/b.z.8. 36/A.28.b.28.	7.		Company scattered Infantry move into billets on LE PETIT MORTIER STEENWERK Road.	CRE
	8.		All available personal employed on repair of roads at LE PETIT MORTIER. Offensive patrols carried arounded.	CRE
	9.		Company employed on construction of bridge repair of road between LE PETIT MORTIER & STEENWERK. Salvage of Timber for operations etc.	CRE

Army Form C. 2118.

WAR DIARY
or
INTELLIGENCE SUMMARY

229TH FIELD COMPANY R.E. 40 DIVN.

SEPTEMBER 1918. (Erase heading not required.)

MAP 36. FRANCE SHEET 36. 1/40,000.

Place	Date	Hour	Summary of Events and Information	Remarks and references to Appendices
LE PETIT MORTIER 36/A.28.b.2.8	9/10		Company employed on bridges and repair of roads etc. as on 9th. Marking out track commenced from B 25c 80.65 to B 22b 2.0.	C.A.S.
	11		Company employed on bridges and repair of roads as on 10th. Track through NIEPPE continued	P.A.S.
	12		Company employed on bridges, roads and tracks as on 11th. Road mine at cross roads at PONT DU BAC (G6.c.8.2) located and dismantled.	C.A.S.
	13		Company employed on bridges, roads and tracks as on 12th. Bridge put over BECQUE DE NIEPPE at B22b.1.0. in continuation of track.	P.A.S.
	14		Company employed on bridges, roads and tracks as on 13th. DIPPER BRIDGE strengthened for heavy traffic.	C.A.S.
	15		Company employed on bridges and roads as on 14th : broken in road filled in at night between B16c and d and B23a.	C.A.S.
	16		Company employed on bridges and roads as on 15th. and clearing of culverts and drains.	C.A.S.
	17		Company employed on bridges, roads and culverts as on 16th.	C.A.S.

Army Form C. 2118.

WAR DIARY
or
INTELLIGENCE SUMMARY.

(Erase heading not required.)

229TH FIELD COMPANY R.E. 40 DIVN.

SEPTEMBER 1918.

MAP 36. FRANCE SHEET 36. 1/40,000.

Place	Date	Hour	Summary of Events and Information	Remarks and references to Appendices
LE PETIT MORTIER	18		Company employed on bridges, roads and culverts as on 17th.	O.H.S.
	19		Company employed on bridges, roads and culverts as on 18th.	O.H.S.
36/A28b28	20		Company employed on billets, and roads and culverts as on 19th.	O.H.S.
	21		Company employed on billets, roads and culverts as on 20th.	O.H.S.
	22		Company employed on erecting new Div. Hd.Qrs. billets, repairing roads etc. as on 21st.	O.H.S.
	23		Three sections employed on new Div. Hd.Qrs. together with Works Company. Remainder of Company on billets and notice boards for Cross Roads and buildings in the Sector.	O.H.S.
	24		Work continued on new Div.Hd.Qrs. and making and erection of notice boards. Wiring of STEENBECQUE LINE commenced with party from Support Brigade for instruction.	O.H.S.
	25		Work on new D.H.Qrs. and notice boards, also wiring continued. Work on Baths at A.22.d.H.Q. and A.24.d.2.2. taken over from 231 Field Company.	O.H.S.
	26		Company in Divisional Reserve. Work continued as on 25th.	O.H.S.

Army Form C. 2118.

WAR DIARY
or
INTELLIGENCE SUMMARY

(Erase heading not required.)

229TH FIELD COMPANY R.E. 40 DIV N.

SEPTEMBER 1918

Place	Date	Hour	Summary of Events and Information	Remarks and references to Appendices
			MAP. FRANCE SHEET 36. 1/40,000.	
LE PETIT MORTIER 36/A.28.b.28	27		Sections engaged on construction of Dugouts at QQ2 or A.21.b.0.7. construction of Div Baths - Gumboot store and drying sheds and Soup Kitchen for winter m.q.	aR
	28		Work as on 27th. Instruction in wiring to parties of men in full ease.	aR
	29		Work as on 27.	aR
	30		Work as on 27.	aR
			At H.Q. of 120 Wilts Branch lane have been made and erected during the latter part of the month in the area between Steenwerck & Petit Mortier. Chiefly road & track signs & billet & farm name boards.	
			A R Rayner Capt R.E. 229 Field Co R.E.	

Vol 29

CONFIDENTIAL

WAR DIARY

OF

229th FIELD Co. R.E.

OCTOBER 1918

VOL - 29

Army Form C. 2118.

WAR DIARY
or
INTELLIGENCE SUMMARY.
(Erase heading not required.)

229th FIELD Coy. R.E.   40th DIVISION

OCTOBER 1918.   MAP. FRANCE Sheet 36 1/40,000.

Place	Date	Hour	Summary of Events and Information	Remarks and references to Appendices
Le Petit Mortier A.28.b.2.8.	1.		Company and attached Infantry Works Coy. billetted in farm buildings near Le Petit Mortier. The Company is in Divisional Reserve and has been working on road repair in the STEENWERCK area. Continuation of new Divisional Head Quarters & farm about 1 kilom. W. of STEENWERCK. Construction of Divisional Baths. Preventin' Rooms etc. On Oct. 1st the Enemy retired towards the Old front line system east of ARMENTIERES. This section continued towards in hand. Instructions received to bridge the River Lys at H.2.c.7.85. with Pontoons. Site reconnoitered & pontoon equipment obtained.	028
	2.		Pushed road for work east on following morning. Work on Div. H.Q. etc. continued by two Sections. Construction of Pontoon Bridge at H.2.c.17.85. 2 miles west of ERQUINGHEM. Width of river was 69', depth centre about 10', and banks 5'. The approach to the bridge from the N.W. side was the old slab roadway from H.1.b.9.6. as far as the river bank, ramped down to its N.E. side. This ramp needed little making.	

Army Form C. 2118.

WAR DIARY
or
INTELLIGENCE SUMMARY.
(Erase heading not required.)

229TH FIELD Coy. R.E. 40° DIV.

OCTOBER 1918.

Place	Date	Hour	Summary of Events and Information	Remarks and references to Appendices
FRANCE MAR Sheet 36 I/40,000.	2		On the slab road embankment had already been trumped at this point to give every covering for the tow-path. The continuation of the slab road on the S.E. side of the river had been blown up at H.2.c.30.65 and could n/t be used without alterations. On here was no long hutt and ramp at this side. A slab road was trenched but shown from the S.E. bridge Road to the farm H.2.c.3.6 using timber from the old roadway	app
	3		Work on new Div HQrs Baths etc continued. Road way from S.E. bridge head of Pontoon Bridge erected on 2nd was cleared through to main ARMENTIÈRES road. Orders received to bridge H.17.78 at ERQUINGHEM alongside the site of the permanent bridge at H.A.C.15.40. Pontoon to be supplied by Corps. Some demolitions to SW of these.	
	4		Work on Div HQ etc. continued. Pontoon Bridge at ERQUINGHEM H.A.C.15.40. This was erected parallel to and just East of the remains of the permanent steel Girder bridge (demolished) and German timber trestle bridge a few feet (also destroyed). Width about 10', Depth 10'-15'. The approach to the bridge from the Western side was by the side of the old permanent ramp leading the Girder bridge. This was a road leaving the conduit place a required clearing. In the house way at the far side was an old Conduit stay a permanent road	app

(A9175) Wt W2358/P360 600,000 12/17 D. D. & L. Sch. 52a. Forms/C2118/15

Army Form C. 2118.

WAR DIARY
or
INTELLIGENCE SUMMARY.

(Erase heading not required.)

229th FIELD Coy. R.E. 40th Div.

MAP. FRANCE Sheet 36 /40.000. OCTOBER 1918.

Place	Date	Hour	Summary of Events and Information	Remarks and references to Appendices
Le Petit Mortier A.28.b.2.8.	4		requiring only to be cleared of debris as far as the Main ESTAIRES - ARMENTIÈRES road. Considerable delay was experienced in getting up the Stores - sent by Corps. Ammn. Park Corps. The last portion was only delivered at 6.30 p.m.	O.B.R.
"	5		Work on Div. HQ. continued. One Section sent forward to ERQUINGHEM to erect billets for the Company. Remainder of Company and No.1 Coy attached were employed in clearing the road through ERQUINGHEM & ARMENTIÈRES. One Section Coy HQ remain at Le Petit Mortier. Remainder move forward to ERQUINGHEM. Billeted in ruins of houses.	O.B.R.
ERQUINGHEM H.A.c.6.3.	6		Coy HQ "Transport" move forward to ERQUINGHEM. One Section at Le Petit Mortier continue work on new Divisional HQ. Forward work concentrated on clearing inter mile & known ARMENTIÈRES & NOUVEAU HOUPLINES. The roads were all passed out but held holes up. Several cave pits filled by panning left generally a route was found which needed clearing of debris. Route cleared for traffic to evening.	O.B.R.
"	7		Further work on traffic routes through ARMENTIÈRES. Other routes reconnoitred. Sentries mounted on gates. Employed marking up direction signs & names of all road junctions in neighbourhood of ERQUINGHEM & ARMENTIÈRES. Repairing road for ARMENTIÈRES to CHAPEL d'ARMENTIÈRES.	O.B.R.

Army Form C. 2118.

WAR DIARY
or
INTELLIGENCE SUMMARY.

(Erase heading not required.)

229th FIELD Coy. R.E.   40th DIVISION

OCTOBER 1918.

MAP. FRANCE Sheet 36. /40.000.

Place	Date	Hour	Summary of Events and Information	Remarks and references to Appendices
ERQUINGHEM H.4.c.6.3.	8		Painting of direction notices in ERQUINGHEM - ARMENTIERES area. Repair of roads leading South from ERQUINGHEM. Clearing obstructions from streams to get rid of swamps at R.E. dump (German Pioneer Park) at ARMENTIERES Station taken over. A large quantity of Engineer material had been left here. Timber of all sizes, Cupolas for protected shelters, Fuzines trench boards, dump spikes & nails. No attempt had been made to destroy these.	app
"	9		Work as on 8th. Testing & filling up pumps at water points in ARMENTIERES. Few water cart filling points erected. Destruction of wells.	app
"	10		Work as on 8th & 9th	app
"	11		" " " "	
			Collection of heavy timber and Plating from derelict bridges & barges in ERQUINGHEM & erecting same forwarded to ARMENTIERES dump for future use as forward roads & bridges.	app
"	12		Work as on 11th. Attached Infantry whole Co. inspected by the Divisional Commander.	app
"	13		Work as on 11th.	
"	14		Work as on 11th. Continued. Pontoon bridge at H.2.c.2.5. dismantled and bridging material handed over to 223 Field Co. R.E. for construction of bridge further west.	

WAR DIARY
or
INTELLIGENCE SUMMARY.

229th FIELD Coy. R.E. 40th DIVISION.

Army Form C. 2118.

MAP. FRANCE Sheet 36 1/40.000. OCTOBER 1918.

Place	Date	Hour	Summary of Events and Information	Remarks and references to Appendices
ERQUINGHEM H.9.c.6.3.	15		Repair of forward roads from ERQUINGHEM eastwards. Collection of heavy timber for bridging and planking for roadways.	cor
"	16		Enemy retired from our portion east of ARMENTIERES. Two sections moved up to CHAPELLE d'ARMENTIERES. Work on forward roads.	
"	17		Two sections and Works Company from SILLES in ERQUINGHEM and two Sections from CHAPEL d'ARMENTIERES move up to NOUVEAU HOUPLINES. Tent allotted. 6 Coopers were to get a track road from HOUPLINES to PERENCHIES via 231st Field (C avoid) to building two bridges over blown up culvert at J.1.9.25. The road from HOUPLINES across the old Yo [Ypres?] ham Kout C.22.c.d.+b, C.23.a.o.c. was found to be in very good condition and but little damaged. There was no serious obstacle while reaching demolished culvert at J.1.9.25 which was mended by 231st Field R.E. The unit poured obstacle was the crater at J.8.c.5.9. A demolished was made and the crater half filled in by 4.0 p.m. 2 wagons passed over by 5.0 p.m. The road forward towards WAR BRECHIES was reconnoitred and craters found at VERLING HEM and LACROIX.	9?1

WAR DIARY or INTELLIGENCE SUMMARY

Army Form C. 2118.

(6)

Place	Date	Hour	Summary of Events and Information	Remarks and references to Appendices
PERENCHIES 12.d.7.2	17.		Working parties from the Infantry & Pioneer battalion were arranged for to free up the debris in turning Rue into two section of it further while M Section cared pack forwards. Arrangements made to take up 2 end (inner) lb bridge material for pontoon bridge at ERQUINGHEM H.3.a.	All
"	18.		Coy HQ Transport moved up to PERENCHIES. Pontoon bridge at H.3.a (ERQUINGHEM) dismantled & pontoon trestle kits returned to 231 Fd Coy at La Croix. 2 Section and Works Company taken on Craters at VERLINGHEM and S La Croix. Passage for all Arm Transport made by midday, direct route opened (two arrows) instead of deviation. Two section party on early in morning to WAMBRECHIES to build bridge over the Canal at D.26.d.6.2. This bridge was opened a Pont Levis supported on two brick abutments and two 5ft brick piers giving three spans of approx. 15', 18' & 18' respectively. The girders of the bridge has all been cut with gelatine. It cap & brickwork of one pier has been blown off for about 5 ft and the abutment on the

WAR DIARY
or
INTELLIGENCE SUMMARY.
(Erase heading not required.)

Army Form C. 2118.

Place	Date	Hour	Summary of Events and Information	Remarks and references to Appendices
	18.		Far side (EAST) partially destroyed. The debris was removed by further demolition in the morning, the brick work of the pier corbels down to a solid course of masonry and the broken abutment cleared. A crib work pier was built up to the stump of the demolished pier and a small crib abutment on the demolished abutment. Timber was obtained from a large German timber park in the village. The civilians left behind rendered valuable assistance in hauling up timber. Spike bolts were made in a civilian forge close by. The bridge was opened for traffic at 6:30 A.M. 19.10.17. Max. load 12 tons.	att

Army Form C. 2118.

WAR DIARY
or
INTELLIGENCE SUMMARY.
(Erase heading not required.)

Map France Sheet 36.

Place	Date	Hour	Summary of Events and Information	Remarks and references to Appendices
WAMBRECHIES K.2.b.8.8.	October 18.		During the day the roads forward of WAMBRECHIES through C. MOLIVEL CROIX, ROUBAIX and TURCOING were reconnoitred & found to be in perfect condition with exception of craters at WAMBRECHIES E.27.c.1.5., E.27.c.4.1, E.28.c.3.8, E.29.c.4.3 and craters at canal in L.2 & L.8 where all the bridges were destroyed all the Lock	C.R.E.
	19		gates blown up thus letting the water & rendering pontooning impossible. Got the men to WAMBRECHIES. Company and attached Works Coy billeted in huts in German Pierre Park. Attempts had been made to fire the timber in the dumps but much heavy timber and building material was left intact. Fires were extinguished & further Stores saved. Sundry road repairs through WAMBRECHIES to Le MOLINEL Craters filled in. On the evening of the 18th - 19th the civilian Engineer in charge of roads bridges etc for the town of ROUBAIX organised a party of civilians and built a bridge over the lock walls at L.8.a.5.3. This bridge took the motor traffic until subsequently replaced by a Decauy bridge.	C.R.E.

WAR DIARY
INTELLIGENCE SUMMARY.
(Erase heading not required.)

Army Form C. 2118.

Place	Date	Hour	Summary of Events and Information	Remarks and references to Appendices
WAMBRECHIES 36/K2b88	20		Map FRANCE & BELGIUM Sheets 36 & 37. Two sections available. Company employed on repair road to ROUBAIX, filling of craters etc. One section standing by pier & piers at WAMBRECHIES. One section building new Trinity beam work walls on road between LE MOUVET and ROUBAIX and canal at L.8.a.7.7. Timber for bridge taken from dump at WAMBRECHIES & road keepers made for telegraph poles on site. Span between walls 17'-6". Max. load	
	21		It was decided to dismantle temporary iron swivel at L.8.a.5.3. built by the French Civilian Engineer as the turning of the booms on the sidewalks was very small and although carrying motor traffic the factor of safety was too small. Arrangements were made with M. Henri Lovers for 8 Company to take this Camp whole steel joists from a factory near WAMBR. These also the necessary timber for the bridge were carted to site. All preparation made for rapidly dismantle this bridge & erecting the new one.	O.R.
	22		Timber bridge at L.8. a. 5.3 dismantled and steel girder bridge erected open for traffic in afternoon. Max load 21½ tons.	O.R.
	23		Co. marche to LE MOUVEL do is accumulate in civilian billets. R.E. dump	

WAR DIARY
INTELLIGENCE SUMMARY

Army Form C. 2118.

Map France & Belgium 36 & 37.

Place	Date	Hour	Summary of Events and Information	Remarks and references to Appendices
LE MOLINEL	23.		at WAMBRECHIES. Handed over to C.R.E. representative. Foot bridge alongside steel girder bridge at LT a 53 constructed.	CRE
	24.		Co. attached work for training, resting.	CRE
	25.		Orders received to relieve 223 Field Coy R.E. 31st Div. in the line in PECQ Sector.	
	26.		One section over Transport proceeds to NECHIN 37/H.1.c.7.8. to take over work and accommodation.	
NECHIN 37/H.1.c.7.8.	26.		Company attached to Infantry proceed by road route to NECHIN & relieve 223 Field CoRE. billeted in NECHIN village. Chief works to cover erection of a Welsh Trestle bridge over the River L'ESCAUT at PECQ 1.2.a.33 the main bridge at PECQ was blown up by the enemy in retreating and the WEST abutment was subsequently blown in by a revising party before the relief. Our Infantry are not established on the East side of the river it is unsafe to erect the bridge. Trestles etc prepared.	
	27.		Received that bridge is not to be attempted until enemy retires. Reconnaissance of new site carried out in early morning.	CRE

WAR DIARY
or
INTELLIGENCE SUMMARY.
(Erase heading not required.)

Army Form C. 2118.

Place	Date	Hour	Summary of Events and Information	Remarks and references to Appendices
NÉCHIN 37 H.Q. 7%	27.		Width of water about 45 ft. with a 6 mph current running. The banks on either side are high very steep which will render a cutting necessary for its approach to the trestle bridge. All preparation made.	
	28.		Reconnaissance of East bank of river carried out to select site for trestle/foot bridge. Site selected was to demolished bridge as piece thrown very cf. which though steeply inclined is passable except for cavalry section. A floating pier was constructed a decking prepared during day. Fire material found on site out at night this in Camouflage and/s foot bridge completed.	CRR
	29.		Cs standing by for extra of bridge where required. Slight shelling of NÉCHIN during night.	CRR
	30.		Cs standing by. Slight shelling of village about 0630.	CRR
	31.		Cs standing by. Information received that enemy has probably retired. Preparation made to move off immediately upon further assurance river. Stronger foot bridge erected across debris of old bridge. Enemy infantry in file [illegible] MAJOR R.E. O/C 208th Field Coy	CRR

229th FIELD COY. R.E.

WAR DIARY.

Nov. 1918.

Vol.

SECRET

WAR DIARY or INTELLIGENCE SUMMARY

Army Form C. 2118.

229th FIELD Coy. R.E.

NOVEMBER 1918. Sheet 37 — 1/40,000

Place	Date	Hour	Summary of Events and Information	Remarks and references to Appendices
NÉCHIN H.15.a.0.0.	Nov 1		Company and attached Infantry billeted in NÉCHIN. Company standing by for erection of trestle bridge over River ESCAUT at PECQ when enemy retire. Engaged in training in the meantime.	
"	2		At 9.12 Owing to rise of river level to 5 ½ ft. current pulling decking off foot bridge at PECQ with walled entry. One section sent forward to re-erect the bridge. Extra floats put in and stronger decking fixed.	O.R.
"	3		Foot bridge reported by Infantry to have been broken up & found bridge intact. Scuttles were blown landing bay made simpler and two beams added thereto. Detail further girder bridge erected and great extra for use beds & abutments taken on centreline of permanent bridge site.	O.R.
"	4		Company standing by & training	O.R.
"	5		do	O.R.
			On 13.30 information was received through division on right that the enemy had retired a short front further information regarding front at PECQ awaited from own infantry.	O.R.

Army Form C. 2118.

WAR DIARY
or
INTELLIGENCE SUMMARY

229th FIELD Coy. R.E.

(Erase heading not required.)

Place	Date	Hour	Summary of Events and Information	Remarks and references to Appendices
NECHIN	5th		MAP. BELGIUM Sheet 37 tooo.	
		H15 a.00	Infantry Bdes. report Enemy still holding East bank of ESCAUT (SCHELDT) at PECQ. They require means of increasing communication with far bank. A half pontoon was sent down to PECQ at 17.30. Owing to enemy artillery fire & M.G. obstacle on road the wagon could not be taken right through to the village & the river bank. It was unloaded & pontoon carried through to river at I.2.c.8.3. It was launched down the steep bank & a cable moored across the river to posts on either bank & further moored weights to form a biffer flying bridge.	
"	6		Company training and preparing materials for bridges at PECQ. Sections and Pioneers for working parties carried down to PECQ in readiness.	932
"	7		Information received that an attack was to take place on the morning of 10th across the SCHELDT. In view of this, the Brigade holding the PECQ Sector asked for a strong solid foot bridge the far-seen the river on the site of the old bridge. It was decided to put a timber trestle bridge across as the floating bridge was unsteady and much disliked by its infantry. The material will all be prepared before hand ready for bolting together on the site & erecting without noise. A careful reconnaissance was	932

WAR DIARY
or
INTELLIGENCE SUMMARY.

229th FIELD Co. R.E.

NOVEMBER 1918.

Place	Date	Hour	Summary of Events and Information	Remarks and references to Appendices
	8.		made and material obtained.	
			During the day all material was prepared ready for bolting together on site & was carted down to P.C.Q. in the evening. It had been intended to erect the bridge on the night of the 9"-10" to prevent the enemy from seeing it before it was required for use. On the evening of the 8" orders were received to erect it immediately. The bridge was erected during the night. Owing to the obstruction in the bed of the stream, it was found impossible to get a trestle down in the middle & consequently a floating pier was put in at centre and replaced in the morning by the box Crib of a pontoon moored to the banks which made a firm pathway.	OBL
9"	4:30 A.M		Information was received by wire from the Brigade in the line at 4:30 A.M. that their patrols had crossed the bridge at P.C.Q. and found that the enemy had evacuated his positions. The battalions were proceeding across the Sheldt. The Company was immediately turned out in fighting order, served with breakfast and marched	OBL

WAR DIARY or INTELLIGENCE SUMMARY

Army Form C. 2118.

229th FIELD Coy R.E.

NOVEMBER 1918

Place	Date	Hour	Summary of Events and Information	Remarks and references to Appendices

down to PECQ. The two Companies of Pioneers who had been standing by in MÉCHIN during the preceding days were warned to move their four Welden Trestles and two Pontoon Superstructure were taken down to PECQ. The site of the new bridge was fixed about 100° North of the permanent bridge site as the approach ramps were easier out on either side & the two Companies of Pioneers employed on constructing the ramps or. Two Sections of Sappers were employed in constructing the Pontoon bridge. One Section of Sappers were sent across the river to assist in making up to road ways on the East side. The fourth Section was led down the main road across the river to fill in the craters which had been blown by the enemy. A mounted reconnaissance party with an officer in charge pushed on ahead to obtain information on the state of the roads etc.

As the river had risen several feet during the last few days it was not necessary to take the ramps as low as had been expected. The ramps were made good with timber & rubble & which road was the bridge opened

CWR

WAR DIARY
or
INTELLIGENCE SUMMARY.
(Erase heading not required.)

Army Form C. 2118.

Place	Date	Hour	Summary of Events and Information	Remarks and references to Appendices
PECQ 37/I.b.99.	10		for traffic at 1930 hours. Section across Shelds: at Pontoon Bridge. Work on repairing decus the marshes on East side of SHELDT continued.	
	11		Deviation round all the craters had been completed on 10th. Work was concentrated on filling in the craters. Orders received for Company to remain in PECQ. Work on road way clean marshes continued. Orders received at 08.30 that hostilities would cease at 1100. Work on roadway continued.	
	12&13		Work as on 11th	
	14		Company resting. Orders received to move back to Le MOLINEL and construct a Pony bridge (for Class D loads) over the Canal at 36/L.i.d.0.5.	

WAR DIARY
INTELLIGENCE SUMMARY.
(Erase heading not required.)

Army Form C. 2118.

Place	Date	Hour	Summary of Events and Information	Remarks and references to Appendices
PECQ.	15.		when retreating LILLE road CRAPS Canal and permanent bridge has been destroyed by the Enemy during his retreat.	
LE MOLINEL	16		Company parade & move off at 06.30 hrs. Billetted in LE MOLINEL. Survey of bridge made and scheme submitted to CRE Division	A.2.
36/F.22683	17		Sunday. All work ceased by order of Division. After Church Service in the fields were organised for the men. Have given 10 places of interest in the neighbourhood.	A.3.
	19		Scheme has been approved for timber girder bridge material was transported from WAMBRECHIES and footing for trestle & exit piers prepared. For details of bridge see attached sketch.	
	18 – 23		Company employed on construction of bridge. The only difficulty experienced was the supply of bolts. These had all to be made by hand & the facilities for so doing in a Field Company R.E. are very small. Tools were borrowed from civilians - this work organised in shifts.	
	24.		Sunday. Church Service [?].	

Army Form C. 2118.

WAR DIARY
or
INTELLIGENCE SUMMARY.
(Erase heading not required.)

Place	Date	Hour	Summary of Events and Information	Remarks and references to Appendices
LE MOULINEL	26 1/30		Work continued on bridge. Two girders completed on 30rd.	A.91
			Educational Scheme	
			In connection with the Educational Scheme organised by G.H.Q. classes were arranged during the month in Civil & O.E. Engineering and Electrical Engineering. Classes were also arranged in Arithmetic, Algebra, Geometry, Practical Mathematics, French Book-keeping, etc. but could not be properly started until arrival of textbooks on the subjects. No 5/5/S.S. Maps could be obtained. Games Tournaments were also organised & facilities given for attendance at lectures at Rouen on Demobilisation & also one on "Exploration" by Sir Francis Joung (husband).	

O.B. Bayos Capt R.E.
OC 129 Field Co. R.E.

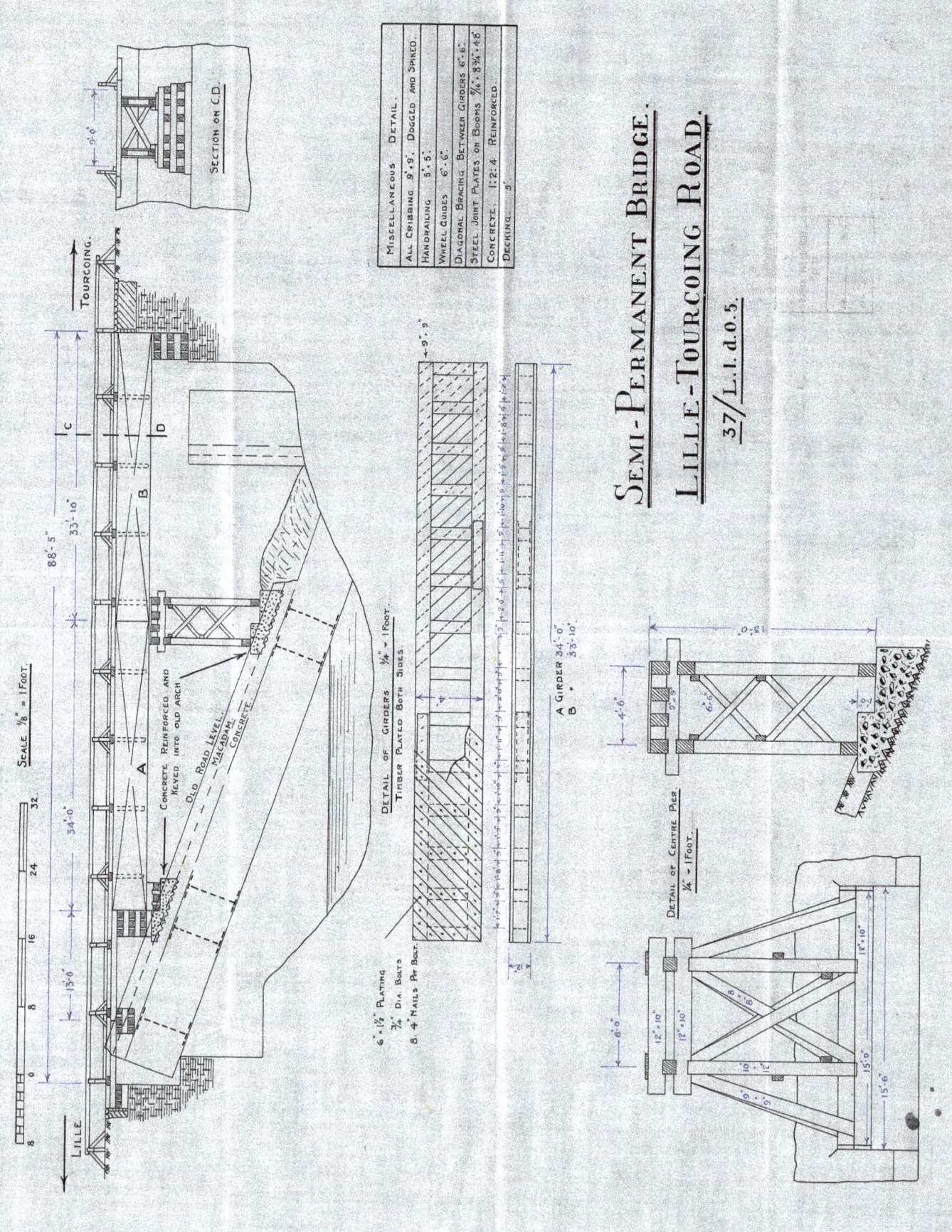

WR 31

Vol.

War Diary
229th Field Company R.E.
December 1918

SECRET

Army Form C. 2118.

WAR DIARY
or
INTELLIGENCE SUMMARY. 229th FIELD Co. R.E.

(Erase heading not required.)

Place	Date	Hour	Summary of Events and Information	Remarks and references to Appendices
Le Molinel	1		Map. BELGIUM & FRANCE. Sheet 36 1/40,000. Company billeted in LE MOLINEL and working under C.E. XV Corps on Construction of Semi Permanent lorry bridge over the Canal de la Deule with Nov. War Diary.	See plan
E.25.c.5.4			TOURCOING - LILLE Road at L.1.d.0.5. Work resumed to complete by 3rd inst.	War Diary
	2		Work as on 1st	do
	3		Bridge Completed and opened for traffic.	do
	4		Company resting — Games etc organised.	do
	5		do	do
	6		do	do
	7		do	
	8		Church Parade. Games etc organised.	do
	9		Erection of huts for R.E. Training School at WAMBRECHIES. Working hours reduced to 0800 — 13.00 Games organised for afternoon.	do
	11		Educative lectures carried on in Evening	do
	12		Subjects Engineering Electrical and Mechanical Mathematics	
	13			

WAR DIARY
INTELLIGENCE SUMMARY

(Erase heading not required.) 229 Field Co R.E.

DECEMBER 1918.

Army Form C. 2118.

Place	Date	Hour	Summary of Events and Information	Remarks and references to Appendices
LE MOLINEL	14		Work etc as on 13.	A(21)
F.25.c.5.A.	15.		Church Parade.	A(31)
	16		Daily Inspection carried out. Billet inspection etc.	
	17		Various small R.E. works carried out — Erection of Divisional	A(5)
	18		baths, repair of Officers buildings etc. Repair of	
	19		hand portable Engines and Threshing machines.	
	20			
	21		Board of Inspection held for all Mobilisation Equipment.	A(32)
	22		Church Parade.	
	23		Erection of Prisoners of War Cage at WAMBRECHIES.	
	24		Repair work etc as above	
	25		General holiday.	A(31)
	26			
	27		Inspection of bridges in area. Company made responsible for maintenance	
	28		of all temporary bridges in area. All bridges Elsewhere	A(31)
			well and not in need of repair.	

Army Form C. 2118.

WAR DIARY
or
INTELLIGENCE SUMMARY.

(Erase heading not required.) 229 Field Coy RE

December 1917

Place	Date	Hour	Summary of Events and Information	Remarks and references to Appendices
LE MOLINEL	29		No work carried out.	
F.26.C.5.4	30		Inspection of bridges. Repair of divisional	
	31		Theatre in ROUBAIX.	GBR

Blanes
Capt RE
OC 229 Field Coy RE
31.12.19

WAR DIARY

OF
229 Field Co. RE

January 1919

Volume 32

Army Form C. 2118.

WAR DIARY
or
INTELLIGENCE SUMMARY. 229th FIELD Coy. R.E.
(Erase heading not required.)

JANUARY 1919.

Instructions regarding War Diaries and Intelligence Summaries are contained in F. S. Regs., Part II. and the Staff Manual respectively. Title pages will be prepared in manuscript.

Place	Date	Hour	Summary of Events and Information	Remarks and references to Appendices
LE MOLINEL F.25.c.54.			MAP. BELGIUM & FRANCE Sheet 36 1/40,000	
	1		Company billeted in Le Molinel. Engaged on erection & repair of Divisional Bath, erection of hutting, repairing threshing machines & engines & general work.	992
			1 O.R. demobilized	992
	2		Capt A.B. Ray re. attached to 5th Army H.Q.	92
	4		Erection standard hut for 119th Inf. Bde. at CROIX journée reprise d'achte.	92
		8R	1. O.R. demobilized	93
		11R	Lieut C.R. Bond and 1 O.R. demobilized. Belgian Croix de Guerre	92
			awarded to 554379 a Cpt COUCHMAN and 105246 CPL G. GRAY	92
	13R		4 O.R. demobilized	92
	16R		3 O.R. demobilized	92
	19R		3 O.R. demobilized	92
	20R		6 O.R. demobilized	92
	21R		5 O.R. demobilized	92
	22		3 O.R. demobilized	92
	25R		2 O.R. demobilized Sections 1 and 2 amalgamated & form one	92
			Section and 3 and 4 ditto do	92

Army Form C.2118/15

Army Form C. 2118.

WAR DIARY
or
INTELLIGENCE SUMMARY.

(Erase heading not required.)

229th Field Coy. RE

Place	Date	Hour	Summary of Events and Information	Remarks and references to Appendices
			MAP BELGIUM AND FRANCE SHEET 36 1/40,000	
LE MOLINEL	26th		5 O.R. demobilized. Lieut P.T. EASTON awarded the M.C. 33163	M.C.
F.25c.54.	27th		Sgt. J. MORTROP mentioned in despatches. New year honours	M.C.
	28		8 O.R. demobilized	M.C.
	29		10 O.R. demobilized	M.C.
	30		14 O.R. demobilized	M.C.
	31		—	M.C.

Mlake? Lt
229 Field Coy RE.

Confidential

Vol 33

War Diary

229th Field Coy. R.E.

February 1919.   VOL 29

Army Form C. 2118.

WAR DIARY
or
INTELLIGENCE SUMMARY.
(Erase heading not required.)

229TH FIELD COY. R.E.

FEBRUARY 1919

Place	Date	Hour	Summary of Events and Information	Remarks and references to Appendices
LE MOUNEL	1/2/19		SHEET 36 1/40,000.	
I.25.c.5.4	2		5 O.R. Demobilized	R.W.B
	3		4 O.R. Demobilized	R.W.B
	6		7 O.R. Demobilized	R.W.B
	7		Major J.W. Playle M.C., R.E. + 7 O.R. Demobilized	R.W.B
CROIX I.9.d.0.3	8		1 O.R. Demobilized - Dismantle pontoon Maroc C. CROIX	R.W.B
	9		3 O.R. Demobilized.	R.W.B
	15		10 O.R. Demobilized	R.W.B
	16		Capt. J.Y. Vose R.E. posted from 131st Fd Cy R.E.	R.W.B
	17		Lieut. J.P. Willis R.E. Demobilized	R.W.B
	20		Construction of bridge over railway at ROUBAIX Station taken over from 13 Fd Cy R.E.	R.W.B
	21 to 28		Lieut. P.T. Easton M.E. R.E. Demobilized	R.W.B
			Party of Coy working on bridge at ROUBAIX Station	R.W.B

R.W. Bolt
Major
229 Fd Coy R.E.

WAR DIARY.

229th FIELD Coy. R.E.

MARCH 1919

Army Form C. 2118.

WAR DIARY
or
INTELLIGENCE SUMMARY.
(Erase heading not required.)

229 FIELD Co. R.E.

MARCH 1919.

Place	Date	Hour	Summary of Events and Information	Remarks and references to Appendices
CROIX L.S.b.o.3.	1 to 17 inclusive		All available personnel employed on billet repairs at ROUBAIX.	S.S.V.
	17		Capt. A.B. Raymer transferred to 224 Field Co. R.E.	S.S.V.
	18 to 22	"	All available personnel employed on billet repairs at ROUBAIX.	S.S.V.
	22		35 O.R. Demobilised.	S.S.V.
	23 to 28	"	All available personnel employed on Coy; wagons cleaning & repairing & painting, and disinfecting, cleaning & packing unused harness.	S.W.
	28		2 O.R. demobilised.	S.S.V.
	29 to 31	"	All available personnel employed on Coy; wagons & harness, cleaning & painting.	S.S.V.

John Bennett Voce
Capt R.E.
O.C. 229 Field Co. R.E.

W.R. 35

229th Field Co. RE.

April 1919.

War Diary.

Vol.

SECRET

Army Form C. 2118.

WAR DIARY
or
INTELLIGENCE SUMMARY.

(Erase heading not required.)

APRIL. 1919.

229 Field Co: R.E.

Instructions regarding War Diaries and Intelligence Summaries are contained in F. S. Regs., Part II. and the Staff Manual respectively. Title pages will be prepared in manuscript.

Place	Date	Hour	Summary of Events and Information	Remarks and references to Appendices
CROIX. L.9.b.o.3.	1st to 5th		All available personnel employed on cleaning + disinfecting surplus harness + Coy. Guards.	9.S.V.
	6th		Church parade.	9.S.V.
	7th-12th		All available personnel employed on cleaning + overhauling Company equipment + repairs to billets in Div: area + Coy. Guards.	9.S.V.
	13th		Church parade.	9.S.V.
	14th-19th		Same as 7th to 12th	9.S.V.
	20th		Church parade. Lt. ROLFE to ENGLAND on leave.	9.S.V.
	21st		All available personnel employed in drawing stores from R.E. Dump + Coy. Guards.	9.S.V.
	22nd		All available personnel employed in removal of Coy. Transport to new Park + Coy. Guards.	9.S.V.
	23rd-30th		All available personnel employed in improvement of billets in Coy area + overhauling Coy. Equipment + Coy Guards.	9.S.V.

John Carruthers
Capt. R.E.
O.C. 229 Field Co. R.E.

9/1836

WAR DIARY

229ᵀᴴ FIELD Coy. R.E.

Vol. _____

MAY 1919

SECRET

Army Form C. 2118.

WAR DIARY
or
INTELLIGENCE SUMMARY.
(Erase heading not required.)

229 FIELD Co. R.E.

MAY. 1919.

Place	Date	Hour	Summary of Events and Information	Remarks and references to Appendices
CROIX.	1st	2.0 to 5.8	All available personnel employed on Coy. Regimental Duties + billet repairs.	S.S.V.
	2nd		Do. do. 6 O.R. demobilised	S.S.V.
	4th 10 to 16		Cadre employed as from 1st to 8th	S.S.V.
	17th		Do. do. (2 O.R. attached to XV Corps for duty	S.S.V.
	18th to 23		Do. do.	S.S.V.
	24th		Do. do. (3 O.R. despatched to army of occupation).	S.S.V.
	25 to 29		Do. do. (2 O.R. rejoined from XV Corps)	S.S.V.
	30 to 31		Do. do.	S.S.V.
	4-11-18 to 25		Church parade.	S.S.V.

John Barnett Voe
Capt R.E.
O.C. 229 Field Co. R.E.

WAR DIARY
or
INTELLIGENCE SUMMARY

Army Form C. 2118.

229 FIELD Co: R.E. (Erase heading not required.)

JUNE. 1919.

Place	Date	Hour	Summary of Events and Information	Remarks and references to Appendices
CROIX	1st-2nd		All available personnel employed on Coy duties.	S.S.V.
L.b.O.S.	3		" " & loading in Mob: Stores.	S.S.V.
	4-7		" " & Billet repairs in Div; area	S.S.V.
	8		" " & Church Parade.	S.S.V.
	9th		" " & cleaning up billets & handing	S.S.V.
	10th		in Coy: Wagons + Bridging Equipment. Capt. Arthur. 25 O.R. demobilised.	S.S.V.
	11th		I.O. + 10. O.R. demobilised (Unit broken up.)	S.S.V.

John Garrutori
Capt R.E.
O.C. 229 Fd. C. R.E.

www.ingramcontent.com/pod-product-compliance
Lightning Source LLC
Chambersburg PA
CBHW081526160426
43191CB00011B/1694